THE YOUNG TERRORIST

ARMINLEAR

Library of Congress Control Number: 2022940222

ISBN (paperback): 978-1-956450-29-3
(eBook): 978-1-956450-30-9

Armin Lear Press Inc
215 W Riverside Drive, #4362
Estes Park, CO 80517

THE
YOUNG
TERRORIST

JOURNEY FROM ARAB MILITANT
TO PROUD AMERICAN

NABIL KHOURI

ARMINLEAR

CONTENTS

1
JOINING AN ARAB MILITIA

"DEATH TO ISRAEL!" I chanted with fellow members of my Arabic Liberation Front (ALF) militia at a rally in Mafraq, our desert hamlet in northernmost Jordan. "Death to America!"

The rallies were exhilarating for this proud eleven-year-old, his prized Russian automatic gun hanging on his shoulder. As a boy whose parents had been forced to evacuate their home when Israel declared itself a sovereign state in 1948, I felt like a man as I cheered against the Israelis alongside others in our Palestine Liberation Organization (PLO) faction. I felt emboldened holding the AK-47 Kalashnikov weapon I would use when we ultimately went to war to reclaim our homeland. Now it was time to head home to bask in the glory.

But about thirty feet from my house on this July day in 1969, I felt a savage kick to the back of my legs. I fell instantly onto my back. Within seconds, two men sat on top of me. One was on my chest; the other strad-dled my waist. Two others stood over me with devil eyes, laughing, their black boots near my head. All four wore scarves to conceal their faces, with only their eyes exposed. I couldn't recognize any of them. They weren't members of the ALF.

Suddenly, the men stopped laughing, and one of them asked, "How does it feel to be a traitor and spy for Israel?"

I remained silent. He asked again, in a louder voice, "You, a brother of a whore, I asked you a question, and you must answer, or I am going to kill you!"

I replied that I was not a spy for Israel or anyone else. "I am a martyr just like you are," I said. "We are brothers. We must fight together shoulder to shoulder. I beg you not to hurt me."

All four men laughed again. Then the one sitting on my waist said, "If you don't want to admit that all ALF members are spies for America and Israel, do you want to admit at least that you are all faggots?" I didn't say any-thing. I felt helpless, almost paralyzed. I wanted to reach for my Kalashnikov, but my arms were pinned against my body. I struggled for air. Then the man sitting on my chest asked me, "Why don't you answer about being a spy and a faggot? Didn't your whore Mama teach you to respond when somebody asks you a question?"

I went crazy when he called my Mama a whore. I told him, "Motherfucker, leave my Mama out of this!" The man grabbed my neck with both hands and pressed fiercely. He was trying to kill me. It became difficult to breathe.

MORE THAN FIFTY YEARS LATER, it all seems like these things happened to somebody else. This person felt an invigorating sense of power from having a Kalashnikov by his side, a belt filled with grenades around his waist, and hundreds of bullets hanging from an old leather strap slung over his left shoulder. Who was this boy that walked the streets of Mafraq, shouting, "If my finger were an Israeli or an American, I would cut it off!" Had I known I would move to the United States eight years later, marry an American woman, give up my Arab nationality to become an American citizen, and form intimate friendships with American Jews, I would have shot myself in the head.

From the moment I was born in 1958, I lived in an environment filled with hatred for the Jews who had settled in Palestine after World War II and for Americans and Britons who helped them move there from displaced persons camps across Europe. When I was little, my *Baba* (father) convinced me that Americans and Jews were our enemies. It's not much of an exaggeration to say I learned the words "I hate Israel" and "I hate America" before I learned to say "Mama" and "Baba." My Baba was jailed for six months around the time I was born for the crime of openly expressing his belief that Jordan's King Hussein was not firm enough with Israel.

My parents lived in Haifa until Great Britain granted sovereignty to Israel in 1948. Baba worked as a physician's assistant with the British army in Haifa before it vacated Palestine. When my Baba was transferred to another British army unit in the Jordanian town of Mafraq, near the Syrian border, my parents had no choice but to relocate.

Mama and Baba loved the house where they lived in Haifa, particularly the orange tree in the backyard. Although my parents were Lebanese Christians and lived in Palestine for only five years, they had developed passionate feelings toward that sacred land. They missed the climate of Haifa and the liveliness of being in a city. Its weather was heaven compared to that of Mafraq. Wintertime was freezing in Mafraq, yet with no snow. In the summer, the temperature reached 100 degrees; nary a drop of rain fell from April to October. The town and its environs were an endless desert, filled with collections of stones and sandstone hills. The nearby low mountains contained little vegetation.

In Mafraq at the time, the majority of the twenty thousand people were Jordanian Bedouins, nomadic people who mostly lived out of tents. Camels, horses, and donkeys were their primary source of transportation, and sheep were their sustenance. The remainder of the population included Jordanian Christians and those thrown out of Palestine like my parents.

I can remember my antipathy toward Israel growing when I was only three years old. I began to overhear conversations between more aged members of my community that Israel should never have existed. As I grew a little older, my parents told me how the U.S. government had initiated an agreement with the British government to give out visas to thousands of Jewish refugees to enter Palestine. I grew up hating Americans for putting this proposal forward and considered the two countries partners in an unjust cause.

My fifth birthday present was a toy gun my Baba bought me. He told me, "Here, this is for you, Nabil. You can shoot the Jews who took over Palestine from us." I grabbed the toy in both hands, raised it, aimed it at my Mama in the kitchen, and began making shooting noises. My dad stopped me and said, "No, no, she is not Jewish. You're only supposed to shoot Jewish people." I paused for a few moments. I looked around for Jews and aimed the toy gun at my siblings, not finding any. I pretended to shoot each of them repeatedly for several months before accidentally dropping my gun and breaking it. However, I felt I was ready to carry a real gun and fight the Jews.

So it was only natural that I joined the ALF at the age of eleven as one of the youngest members. Besides shining my leader's boots at a moment's notice, one of my primary responsibilities was to ensure that the newspapers in the bathroom at ALF headquarters did not contain pictures of our esteemed chairman, Yasser Arafat. We would sit just outside the bathroom and tear out all the pictures of Chairman Arafat. Then we neatly folded the photos and placed them inside a brown bag that hung on a hook in the kitchen. Approximately ten other members of my militia group were preteens like me with similar responsibilities. There were also 50 teenagers, and 140 members between 20 and 50 years old.

Those joining a militia group were strictly volunteers except for our leaders, who received payment from the PLO. Enrolling with any Palestinian militia group in the late sixties was easy. You just had to be male and older than ten.

It took me less than ten minutes to sign up as an ALF member in early May 1969. I was interviewed by two ALF members, one of whom was my age and the other about twenty years old. The interview occurred on the street just outside ALF headquarters, where they asked my name, religion, and age. They scribbled down my name and told me to come back Friday for a rally to pick up a Kalashnikov, uniform, belt, and boots.

I felt as if I could fly. The idea of carrying a rifle in the streets of Mafraq thrilled me. I would be powerful and in control now—a man, not a boy.

Although the objective of the ALF, as with every militia organization in Mafraq, was to liberate Palestine from the Israelis, I had a personal goal besides politics. I wanted desperately to fit in with Jordanian society. I was weary of the Jordanian Muslim children mocking me for being Lebanese. I tried to stop the kids who threw rocks at me and made fun of my Lebanese background and accent. They said I sounded like a girl and made snide comments like, "Go back to your country. We don't want strangers on our land. Christians don't belong in Muslim countries."

Christians were in the minority across the Middle East and historically had been discriminated against by Muslims. Many Arabs viewed my countrymen as cowardly because Lebanon, which was the only peaceful country in that region, refused to participate in the Six-Day War against Israel in 1967. As a member of the ALF, I was going to stop the Jordanian children's hurtful comments about me and my native country.

I could hardly wait for the Friday rally to arrive. I kept my ALF membership a secret from everyone, including Mama, my most trusted friend. I wanted to make it a complete surprise for her and my siblings. I was very disappointed my dad was out of the country, working as a physician's assistant in a Saudi Arabian hospital, and couldn't be there for my big day. He had left us in March 1967, three months before the war, on a three-year contract. From the day he departed, I did not know when I would see him again.

I hardly slept the night before the rally as I thought of myself carrying a gun like all the other militia members. I woke up early that morning. Making sure to be quiet, I sneaked out of the house and walked toward ALF headquarters. A part of me was delighted, but another was anxious. My legs were practically shaking. I began to sweat like I was performing hard labor. I told myself I shouldn't be scared. After all, I was only minutes away from being a source of terror to other people. I loved the idea and told myself I would enjoy the attention. I arrived at headquarters at 5:00 a.m. on Friday, May 9.

At least twenty members were sitting on the courtyard's ground with their guns next to them. As I entered the building, five of them climbed to their feet and aimed their Kalashnikovs toward me. I froze, speechless. I was so frightened I forgot the reason for my visit. Suddenly, one man still seated pointed his index finger at me and said, "Oh yeah, I know you. You registered with us last week. Today is your first day." The word "relief" was beyond an understatement.

He asked me to follow him to the conference room. My heart beat as fast as if I were running a race; my palms turned sweaty as I entered the room and saw it half-filled with uniforms, guns, and boots. Next, he handed me a uniform and said, "Here, put it on." I felt like I was dreaming. Once I had it on, he picked up a belt with bullets and tied it around my waist. "I must be in heaven. I must be in heaven," I kept telling myself. Then he gave me a pair of boots and ordered me to put them on.

Once I was done, he handed me what I had been waiting for—the Kalashnikov. I was overjoyed. I felt complete and satisfied for once in my life. I felt relieved, too, as if I had been in a desert for days without water, and suddenly it started pouring rain. I kept thanking the man repeatedly. I couldn't think of anything to say except "thank you, sir, thank you, sir." I wanted to show my gratitude in any way possible. I gladly would have been his slave for the rest of my life to repay such kindness and generosity for giving me all the things I needed to become a man, a soldier, a terrorist, and a martyr. I now could kidnap any politician on Earth or hijack a plane. I was going to become a hero and famous. I was going to be on newscasts all over the world. I kissed the old me goodbye and embraced the new.

I reveled in my first rally, feeling pure enjoyment and a sense of machismo at being with my fellow militia members. Some of us shouted pro-militia slogans. We also sang patriotic songs such as:

> *My country, my country, my love, and my heart*
> *belong to you.*
> *Palestine, Palestine, my love and my heart belong*
> *to you.*
> *I am ready to kill and be killed for you.*

Some of us danced and jumped in the streets. A few men shot their guns into the sky. The enthusiasm that surrounded me made me want to go to war. It didn't have to be with Israel. It could be with anyone at all.

I couldn't wait to go home and show my Mama, Fatina, the one I adored, the new me. I wanted her to be proud of her youngest son, to let her see for herself how much I had grown up since the previous evening. I wanted the woman I idolized to give me her blessing for joining the ALF. I also was excited to show my two older brothers and sisters the new me. I wished Aida, my oldest sister, who was 20 years older than me, were there to see me. She was grown and living in Kufranja, Jordan, with her own young family.

I had always been closest to my Mama. In 1969 Mama was forty-nine years old with dark brown hair and black eyes that looked like Lebanese black olives. She stood five feet, seven inches, tall for an Arab woman, and had a heavy build. Her face always had a smile, even during difficult times. She had a hearty, booming laugh that made everyone around her feel better about life. Sometimes I felt as if I were part of Mama. Often I would talk with her through my eyes without saying a word; she was my best friend.

When I arrived home dressed in an ALF uniform, my gun hanging over my right shoulder and a belt with bullets and grenades around my waist, my mother was busy washing dishes in the kitchen sink. I walked into the kitchen and stopped several feet behind her. I was as proud as a victorious soldier just back from battle. I stood there for a moment, but Mama still didn't detect my presence, so I cleared my throat to get her attention. She turned in my direction, and the first thing that caught her eye was my gun. Her reaction was not the one I expected. She became hysterical. Her eyes opened up like saucers. She swallowed hard and began yelling at me.

"How could you do this to me?" she cried. "How could you do this to your siblings? I am so ashamed of your behavior. Who are you planning to shoot with this gun? Me? Your sisters or your brothers? Please, son, I beg you to take all this shit and return it to the militia, for God's sake. You are still too young to become a soldier. If your Baba were here, you would not dare pull this shit on him. I never expected to raise a son to turn out like you. I thought you had more sense than this and cared about your family. Now you proved to me that you are full of lies and are a hypocrite."

I stood completely still in front of her. Watching her cry and seeing her disappointment tore my heart to pieces. Holding back my tears, I said, "Mama, I am very sorry I hurt you, but I had to do this. I need to protect myself from the Jordanian children who keep bothering me. Since my father is gone, I need to protect you and my siblings."

"Protect us from what?" Mama responded, shaking as she continued to shout. "The Israeli warplanes? If all the Arab armies couldn't stop the Israeli Air Force, why do you think you can stop it on your own? Or are you planning to protect us from the Jordanians? They are harmless and kind people. We don't need any protection. We feel safe here even with your dad gone."

I was shocked at Mama's reaction to my new man-hood. I was crushed. I wanted her to be proud of me. Instead, she was angry. I didn't know what to do, so I excused myself and went to bed. Mama insisted I put my Kalashnikov under her bed overnight for safety reasons. I felt empty and naked without it next to me. I hardly slept because I was thinking about my gun the whole night.

Despite my mother's protestations, I decided to

remain with the ALF. I arose at 6:30 in the morning to get ready for school. I stopped by ALF headquarters since it was on my way, just a block from my house and midway between home and school. Once I joined up, I routinely stopped there to or from school.

The building had four separate rooms: the leader's office, a conference room, a kitchen, and a small bathroom. Like many other buildings in Mafraq, headquarters was constructed of a mixture of soil, hay, and gravel. The leader's room, conference room, and kitchen floors were cement; the bathroom floor was raw earth. The leader's office had a desk and two chairs. The conference room contained uniforms, boots, belts, and guns stacked on the floor. The kitchen had pans hung from hooks on the wall, and in the corner stood a gas stove. The ground in the bathroom had a hole about one foot in diameter for discharging our waste. Two pails rested alongside the hole. One was filled with clean newspapers we wiped ourselves with after defacating, and the other with the used ones. We burned the dirty newspapers every evening behind the building. Severe punishment would be inflicted on anyone caught wiping his ass using newspaper with Arafat's picture.

The ALF was one of several PLO organizations in Mafraq in the late 1960s. The PLO factions began to evolve shortly after the 1967 war. Many Palestinians were forced to evacuate their homes as Israel took over the West Bank of Jordan, the Golan Heights of Syria, and the Gaza Strip and Sinai of Egypt. My ALF political party was aligned with the Iraqi government and was financed by its governing Ba'ath Party. Major decisions within the ALF organization had to be approved by both the Iraqi government and the PLO. This was not an unusual circumstance in Jordan, where the various Arab governments financed many Palestinian militia groups to support the fight against Israel.

My militia group was one of the smallest in Mafraq. There were upwards of three thousand guerrillas who belonged to the various militia groups stationed within the one square mile of the town's city limits.

Joining the ALF in 1969 had the desired effect as the children of Mafraq stopped ridiculing my siblings and me and began to respect and fear me. Most Jordanian children looked to the ground with trepidation as I passed them. I explained to each child I saw on the street how my Kalashnikov, which was at my side at all times except at school—where we were prohibited from carrying firearms—was capable of shooting thirty-one bullets in a single round. I aimed it at the child's chest as an added measure of intimidation.

Ninety-nine percent of my fellow soldiers in the various militia organizations were evacuated Palestinians. The remaining 1 percent were either Jordanians or members of other nationalities who felt they were somehow lesser than the Jordanians. I fit in perfectly with the Palestinian militia members. I was a foreigner just like they were, and I had a different dialect, too. The Palestinian militia soldiers never seemed to mind that my accent was unusual even compared to theirs.

Our leaders provided cigarettes for their followers, but I chose not to smoke. I didn't care for the smell. We often received rations of ten sardine cans, five mixed vegetable cans, and one kilogram of rice every Thursday, which was precious to my hungry family. Trucks from PLO headquarters in the Jordanian capital of Amman delivered these items to our Mafraq headquarters every Wednesday night. The ALF also provided us with unique military uniforms that included khaki-colored pants and shirts, and black boots. I loved wearing my uniform: it made me feel older and more manly. We were under no obligation to wear the uniform or boots Saturday through Thursday. But on Fridays, the Muslim holiday, we all had to wear them.

Each Friday, from dawn until dusk, the militia groups gathered their members together in the Mafraq desert to train in target shooting and mock hand-to-hand battles, or they sent them to the city for street rallies. Marching through the streets, we carried the Palestinian flag with three equal horizontal stripes - black, white, and green - and a red triangle.. Militia leaders taught us the meaning of each color. Black symbolized mourning for all the men who died and sacrificed their lives for Palestine. White represented the purity of the children of Palestine who were thrown out of their country by the Israelis. Green portrayed the land of Palestine, which was filled with vegetation. The red triangle represented all the Palestinian men killed while trying to liberate their land.

We also carried banners with the words "Death to Israel, Death to America" scrawled across them. Sometimes our banners had red paint spots, signifying the bleeding of Palestine. We chanted loudly, "Death to the Israelis! Death to the imperialists and the old societies! Death to America! Victory to the Palestinians! God bless our chairman, Yasser Arafat. God is great. God bless Abu Ammar." Abu is the prefix to a name that represents the Palestinian revolution, so, like Arafat—whose revolutionary name was Abu Ammar—we each created our revolutionary names. Mine was Abu Khaled.

Each militia organization had a separate leader who worked for a specific political group or party. In some cases, our leaders were rivals, which often resulted in our respective militias fighting each other on Jordanian soil. During these rallies, the ALF clashed with an opposing group called the Syrian Sahaka Revolution, which received its finances and orders from the Syrian government. The Sahaka organization was stronger militarily than our party, with several hundred members. Their fighters received superior training and more gun power. I went home with a bruised and battered body a few times after skirmishes with the Sahaka.

The rallies at the market were memorable. They were held in Mafraq's only market, a series of adjoining shops along one paved road. Most Jordanians who owned the shops stood outside and waved at us, while others were satisfied with a simple smile. All the shop owners were male. An unwritten rule specified that only men were allowed in the marketplace. Women were not supposed to shop or even stand next to men in Mafraq.

The shop owners wore typical Jordanian garb; an ankle-length free-flowing cotton gown called the *thobe*. Over this garment, some wore a sleeveless coat of cotton, wool, or camel hair called the *abah*; which could be made of silk in the summer months. They also wore a scarf on their heads, called a *keffiyeh*. It was cotton cloth with a white or checkered pattern that was folded in a triangle and placed on the head so the middle point hung in the back and the two ends came over the shoulders. It was held in place by a coil of black cord that was called the *agal*.

The Jordanians remained silent during our demonstrations, but we could see the pain associated with an uncertain future caused by our militias' presence. The Jordanians, by this time, had become fully aware of the numbers and capabilities of the Palestinian militia groups in Mafraq. They felt hopeless and helpless every time a Palestinian rally took place, driving away customers.

The Jordanians did like hearing us declare, "Death to Israel." They hated Israel as much as we did. After all, Israel was the reason the Palestinians were in Jordan in the first place, slowly taking over the country from Jordanian control. But they were paying the price for our presence and disliked it.

One of our rallies took place in July 1969. This one would be different than the rest for me. Usually, after rallies, most of us went back to the ALF headquarters for an hour or so before going home to brag about our event. That evening, I decided to go home directly after the rally. I wasn't feeling very well. My throat hurt from all the chanting. I left feeling exhausted and thirsty with my Kalashnikov fitting snugly on a strap by my side as if it were part of my body. Suddenly, the four attackers appeared.

THE ATTACKER'S GRIP ON MY THROAT TIGHTENED, and I feared he would choke me to death. In my ALF militia training, I learned not to accept death from a ruthless enemy easily. I had to find a way to fight and give them hell before they killed me. Although I could not see the four men's faces, I knew they were members of the Sahaka. Who else would hate an ALF member so much?

I worked up my courage and grabbed my tormentor's hands hard, sticking one of his fingers inside my mouth. I bit it with a force I didn't know I had. I continued biting his finger with all the strength I could muster. I felt and heard the crushing of the bones of his finger between my teeth. The man screeched, but it did not deter me. His finger began to bleed inside my mouth. I tasted his blood, and I loved the flavor. It made me wild. I was thirsty for it. It turned me into a desert wolf.

Pain overwhelmed the man. He kept howling at his

companions who stood over me, commanding them to "Shoot him, shoot him, he is biting off my finger!" He finally let my neck go, but I wouldn't let go of his finger. He tried to get off my chest, but he didn't get far with his finger still nailed between my teeth. The man's three friends were in utter disbelief when they saw my mouth filled with their companion's blood. The man who was about to lose his finger shouted, "I am going to kill you, I am going to kill you!"

The man sitting on my waist got up and kicked me in the stomach. I felt as if a knife had been stuck inside me. The pain shooting through my body made me open my jaw long enough for the nearly severed finger to drop. All four men began kicking me in the stomach and chest. A strange noise like a deep cough came from my mouth each time they kicked me. I was just about to pass out. I wished they would shoot me in the head and finish me off. The last kick was leveled at my nose. Instantly, blood flowed from both nostrils like a faucet. Their shrieking filled my ears as they continued kicking me.

Suddenly, they stopped and started running away. I thought they had shot me.

I didn't comprehend what was happening. I didn't know if I was still alive when I saw the shadows of two men standing over me. I thought they were the angels of death. I looked more closely as they advanced toward me and lifted me. They were not angels exactly, but my Jordanian neighbors who rescued me. They put their lives in danger to save me from the Palestinians with whom I had become allied to force the Jordanians to respect me. They carried me home and took me to my Mama.

When Mama saw my face, she almost fainted. She ran to the kitchen and brought towels and a pail filled with water. Crying uncontrollably, she began washing my face. Mama laid me on my back on the kitchen floor for a few minutes while she stopped the blood spewing from my nose. Once the bleeding ceased, she helped me sit up halfway and take off my shirt, discovering that my chest was covered with red blotches. The pain in my nose was so searing I couldn't even feel the damage to my chest.

When my Mama finished cleaning my nose, she looked into my eyes for several moments, wiped her tears with her palms and said, "Nabil, son, love, I want you to listen to me. These Palestinian militias are a bunch of unlawful thugs declaring that they want to liberate Palestine. If they wanted to liberate Palestine, shouldn't they be on the border with Israel instead of being here among the Jordanian civilians? If they wanted to kill the Israelis as they claim, why do they keep fighting each other?"

I didn't want to hear what Mama said even though I knew deep down, she was right. I yearned to tell her that the ALF group was a great organization, that we were not unlawful or a group of thugs. However, I was in too much pain to talk. I also couldn't tell her the truth about the ALF and the other militias' ideas of war. I didn't want to frighten her even more. If I left the ALF, they might take revenge by hurting my family or me. So my only choice was to stay with them.

2
DEATH OF A CLASSMATE

THE NEXT AFTERNOON, I limped to ALF headquarters. Struggling, I bent down to sit on the floor of the front courtyard against the kitchen wall: both legs spread out straight ahead, my Kalashnikov resting next to me. I was in severe pain and could hardly talk to anyone. I was so preoccupied thinking about the beating from the previous night that I wasn't in the state of mind to say much anyway.

Even so, I felt comfortable there among the men. I felt secure. Many other members sitting near me chatted as I sat quietly. Two teenage members next to me had cigarettes dangling from their mouths. Finally, I told them about the Sahaka men who had beaten me up. They were not surprised. They said these incidents were expected and had become part of life. If I wanted to become a hero, I needed to get used to it. They added that we should always be alert because the Sahaka traitors could attack us anywhere. I was too weak to respond further and had a hard time even looking their way as my neck was sore. It was just as well. I was embarrassed and didn't want them to see the pain and fear in my eyes. That was the first time I felt any regret for joining the ALF. I could see that I was on a path to hell.

The battles with the Sahaka militia organization did indeed go on. But the chaos was hardly confined to fighting them. There were other militias and foreign forces as well. Within days, before I even had a chance to recover from my beating, death hit so close to home that I awakened further to its insanity.

IT WAS A SKIRMISH BETWEEN two other militias that changed me forever. In late 1969, six months after I joined the ALF, two young boys who lived nearby were killed. One lived two blocks away from our house, and belonged to the Popular Front for the Liberation of Palestine (PFLP), led by George Habash. He founded the organization after the 1967 Arab-Israeli war. Although the PFLP was aligned with the PLO, it was the counterpoint to Al Fatah, the original militia group formed and led by Arafat. The relationship between these two organizations was highly volatile, much like the ALF and the Sahaka.

This particular encounter started when a member of the PFLP accused a member of Al Fatah of spying for the western imperialist countries.

I was with some of the men from my militia group in

Mafraq's desert for training. The desert looked like a brown sea filled with sand instead of water. We were training in white weapons—the term used for knives and swords. By midafternoon we were exhausted, hot, and thirsty. My skin was so wet with sweat that I looked as if I had bathed in salt. Our leader gave us a few minutes break.

We ran to the only water tank, which had a cylindrical shape and three faucets. The tank sat on two wheels and was attached to the rear of a truck. A metal string tied three separate aluminum cups to each faucet. The strings were long enough for the cups to reach from the faucet to our mouths. I stood in one of the lines waiting my turn, desperate for the one drink of water allowed us. If a person needed a second cup of water, he had to go to the end of the line.

After my first cup of water, I felt I could easily use another one or two. I couldn't get them, though, as I needed a bowel movement. I left the crowd and went to a private area to relieve myself. I was wiping myself using specially selected stones with a smooth surface when I heard shooting coming from the direction of Mafraq. I ran back to the men and saw their faces filled with fright and confusion. Some faces looked as red as blood, others as yellow as lemons. A few of the men whistled with fingers in their mouths, blowing three long breaths through their pursed lips. Three long whistles were our signal for an emergency event.

We all jumped to the truck's rear and drove toward

Mafraq, about twenty minutes away. My heart raced, and my sweaty body suddenly turned to ice as I stood in the back of the truck with the other men. I didn't want to go back to town and become involved in another battle. I didn't want to be shot or killed. After my recent beating, I realized what it was like to be in searing pain, gasping for air, and humiliated. Just thinking about that evening made me feel physically and emotionally broken.

As we approached the village, the gunfire became louder. I thought Israeli jets were bombing Mafraq again. My Mama and siblings suddenly entered my thoughts, and I imagined them being shot and killed by the Israelis. As we entered the city limits, the shooting stopped unexpectedly. The town looked as if it had been separated from the rest of the world. There wasn't one living thing on the streets, not even the ever-present wild donkeys. All the windows of the houses were shut with curtains drawn, and the shops were deserted.

When we arrived at ALF headquarters, we saw that ten members who had stayed behind during our desert training were standing outside. They told us they thought the shootings were coming from Mafraq's market, but they didn't know who was involved in the battle. I felt relieved the shooting wasn't from Israeli jets. That meant my family was safe.

Some of us went inside the office. I decided to stay outside. I didn't want to miss anything and needed to be closer to the action. I had my Kalashnikov in my hands, ready for any surprises. Although I was still thirsty and weary from all the training, I portrayed confidence. But I couldn't fool myself or those around me for more than a few minutes. Feeling weak, I had to sit down in the middle of the street, my gun resting comfortably in my lap.

I stared intently at the blue sky as though searching for God. While deep in my thoughts about my dad and how lucky he was to be out of Jordan, I heard screaming and weeping nearby. I scrambled to stand up and looked around. All the men near me wore worried and tense expressions. The commotion became louder and closer, and the only people in the street were our men.

We finally pinpointed the sounds coming from the block behind the ALF building. I began walking in that direction with several men from my group. The crying and shrieking were from women and children. The sounds saddened and frightened me. The women's voices sounded like my mother's, drawing me to them. I imagined my Mama was crying over losing one of her beloved children.

I forced my wobbly feet to keep moving toward the shouting while a few other ALF soldiers trailed behind me. I approached a crowd of people, all with horrified looks, and squeezed between them to find out what happened. Three of my men tried to follow, with one shouting at me to not get too deep inside the crowd. I acted as if I hadn't heard him. I could thread myself more easily through the full-grown men with an eleven-year-old's body.

Soon the men lost track of me, and I realized that

most of the screaming was coming from the Rami family's house, less than two blocks from mine and a half block behind ALF headquarters.

I saw Surraia Rami outside her house wearing a long black dress and bare feet. Mrs. Rami was about forty years old, and short but heavy. Her black hair fell in startling contrast to her pale skin. She was a quiet lady who hardly smiled. Losing her husband to lung cancer when she was in her mid-thirties had made life difficult. Raising her children alone, she cleaned houses to buy food. My Mama knew Mrs. Rami from the church and its activities. She would give her a loaf of bread every couple of weeks to feed her children—she did so more often when Baba worked in Mafraq.

Mrs. Rami was outside her home screeching, sobbing, pulling her hair, and slapping her face brutally with her own hands. She had just lost her youngest son, Adel. I heard her shout, "Please God, return my child to life! Please, God, don't do this to me! Oh shit! Oh, God! What kind of God are you? You are a devil, not God. I hate you! I hate you!"

Mrs. Rami was collapsing when some women enveloped her and dragged her into her house.

Adel, was a classmate of mine. We were the same age. He always wore the same old white T-shirt and gray pants that he inherited from his older brother. Adel had straight black hair, black eyes, and skin that looked naturally tan. He and I constantly argued about who had the better leader and who belonged to the stronger organization. Despite our differences, I used to feel sorry for the poor boy who often came to school hungry because his mom had nothing to feed him. Once he had the flu and complained about his cold and wet feet. His socks and shoes were filled with holes. I took off my socks and shoes and traded them for his. Adel was ecstatic. He looked deeply into my eyes and asked why I was doing this. I smiled and said that you and I live the same hellish life. Mama noticed the old, torn shoes when I walked inside the house. After explaining what I had done, she became angry and told me she didn't have money to buy me another pair of shoes. She said we hardly had food, and I was stupid to give my socks and shoes away. Mama accused me of being an irresponsible, careless child. She said I was selfish and had taken advantage of her. She threatened that if I ever did anything like that again, she would let me go hungry for the rest of my life. Feeling that I had committed a crime, I promised her I wouldn't do it again.

Adel's death astounded me. It made me realize that many of us who belonged to revolutionary organizations were being destroyed by Arab men, not the Israelis. A few days after Adel's death, I wondered if I were the next to be killed by a fellow Arab militiaman.

After Adel's death, I felt close to his soul. I asked his spirit one day in school what it was like to die by the hand of an Arab fighter and not an Israeli. Was the rumor true that when one of us was shot by another Arab revolutionary member, the bullet didn't hurt as much as

27

an Israeli soldier's bullet? I implored my classmate's spirit to forgive me for having such a caustic relationship with him when he was alive.

I opened my heart to his soul. "You and I are basically in the same boat. I know your reason for becoming a member of the PLO organization is the same as mine," I cried. "You were tired of being harassed by the Jordanian Muslim children for being a Jordanian Christian. I wish I had opened my heart up to you when you were alive. After all, you and I were one soul inside two bodies, my friend. Now I am not sure if it was worth it to choose this route to stop the taunting of the Jordanian Muslim children. The children's comments never made us bleed or threatened our lives. Adel, I hope you can hear me. Please rest in peace, my partner. I feel it won't be long before I join you and talk to you because I am following your steps."

A week after Adel's death, his mother committed suicide by overdosing on medication.

Mama and I went to Mrs. Rami's funeral. I had to sit separately from my Mama inside the church. Women usually sat in the left set of pews, and the men in the right. I kept turning in the direction of Mama, who cried throughout the service. Her tears looked like crystal drops falling onto her face.

The priest prayed over the dead woman's body with a trembling sadness. "Today, Surraia left us, last week her child left us, and next week we don't know who will be leaving us."

I looked at Mama as the priest talked and saw her eyes staring at me differently. She didn't seem to see me looking at her. Usually, I could read her eyes, but they were veiled, filled with sadness, anger, and despair. Her eyes, covered with many emotions, could pierce right through me.

After the funeral, I decided to go home. I didn't want to go to the cemetery with the mourners. I'd had enough sadness for the whole week, even enough to last a lifetime. I didn't want to watch Mrs. Rami being buried in the ground.

Mama decided to go home with me. As we left the church Mama said, "Nabil, honey, if you ever get killed by the militia, I will become Surraia the second. If you want to see me go crazy and kill myself, you should continue with the militia. I've had it with you and with the hoodlums you hang around with."

Mama started crying.

"I thought you loved me," she hollered.

Immediately, I answered, "I adore you, Mama."

She asked me, "Then why do you want to see me sad like this? I beg you to leave the ALF tonight. Yes, tonight."

I didn't respond. We both kept walking silently. Once we arrived home, I hurried to my bed, even though it was not bedtime yet. I wanted to be left alone. I stayed awake almost the entire night thinking of Mrs. Rami, Adel, Mama, and life. I was amazed by this existence and how short it could become. As troubled as I was by

Adel and Mrs. Rami's deaths, I couldn't leave the ALF as I was terrified of their revenge.

DURING RALLIES, our battles with the Sahaka kept up in the ensuing days and months. Usually, they began with one member of our group proclaiming that our leader was more patriotic than theirs, or vice versa. The various militia factions were always competing. Each believed it was superior and grabbed any chance to prove it. Our clashes often began with fistfights and fired shots, sometimes killing or injuring militia members. Whenever somebody from our organization died, we all said he was lucky because he went directly to be with Allah in heaven. Death had become a nonevent to us. It was so familiar and close that it had become a part of our lives.

The first time I experienced a battle between the ALF as a group and the Sahaka militia was during a rally in 1969, four months after joining the ALF. The rally began with the usual shouts and bravado. I carried a Palestinian flag like the rest of my militia and chanted, "Death to Israel! Death to America! ALF is going to liberate Palestine! Our leader is the best! Our leader is the only patriotic leader in Mafraq!" One hour after the rally started, we noticed a group of about fifty Sahaka coming toward us. As they approached, we heard them chanting and singing about their leader being the best commander in Mafraq. Their loud voices threatened to drown out ours.

Suddenly, their fighters were wandering into our rally. They were trying to shut us down, to denigrate us. We responded by pushing the invaders away, and in no time, we were wrestling and fist fighting.

The events surprised me, but even more shocking was how calm I remained amid the chaos. I continued walking with the Palestinian flag and my Kalashnikov over my right shoulder. Several times I was pushed, but I rose to my feet every time I fell and moved forward. I saw men kicked and punched in the face, chest, and stomach. Less than five minutes after the fisticuffs began, I heard shooting. Even that did not deter me from proceeding. I was determined to impress upon the fellow militia members that I was a brave soldier despite my youth. Soon I realized the shooting was not toward each other but the sky, a common intimidation tactic.

Finally, we wore the Sahaka down because we outnumbered them, and they began to retreat. Some ran back toward the Sahaka headquarters. We remained in the market street, continuing our rally. It was a good day. No one from either group was killed.

MAFRAQ COULDN'T BE ANYTHING *but* chaotic, given all the various factions of Palestinian fighters within Jordan. Meanwhile, Jordanian soldiers were scarce in Mafraq because most were massed at the Israeli border, so residents ran and hid inside their homes whenever a battle started between Palestinian factions. What other choice did they have given they were largely unarmed while we were equipped with deadly machine guns?

But the situation was even more chaotic because of the presence of the Iraqi military. Shortly after the 1967 war, the Jordanian government officially requested that the Iraqi government send at least twelve thousand men to be stationed in Mafraq's desert. The town was under frequent assault from Israeli air raids.

The Iraqi army had been a welcome sight at first. The Jordanian Bedouins regularly provided them with food and coffee as they felt relieved that a strong army was defending them from the Israelis. Also, the Iraqis stayed out of our militias' conflicts. Their primary function was to fire rockets to bring down attacking Israeli warplanes. The Israelis often turned Mafraq into a miniature hell filled with burning fires that lasted all day and night. Their planes dropped bombs with substances similar to the napalm dropped by the Americans in Vietnam, incinerating anything they touched. When I was in fifth grade, Israeli warplanes flew so low over my school that many of the windows shattered, with glass shards flying over the heads of students sitting in class.

In the beginning, Iraqi soldiers were stationed in the desert just outside Mafraq with their tanks, trucks, heavy equipment, and jeeps. They rarely entered the town except for shopping. However, several weeks after they arrived in the desert, many of the Iraqi units decided to move inside the city limits of Mafraq, where it was more comfortable and closer to shops and markets.

However, they would become a source of hate in the town. Their move into the city angered the Jordanians because it violated the original agreement between the two countries. The Iraqi soldiers quickly began to wear out their welcome.

The Iraqis were crude. They seemed unaware and incapable of civilized behavior. I often saw soldiers unbuttoning their trousers to piss or shit next to city building walls, which heightened the Jordanian's disgust. The Iraqis also completely disregarded Muslim mores regarding women. Jordanian women dressed very conservatively. The women covered their bodies with black dresses and shawls from head to toe. The only thing visible was their eyes, which looked as though a prettier God had created them. Bedouin women's eyes are much larger than the average woman's. Their eyelashes are so thick and long that an eagle could land on them. Harassing one of these women in Muslim society could cost a man his life. Yet several times, I saw Iraqis following Jordanian women down Mafraq streets, harassing them with lewd comments and dirty gestures.

On several occasions, I saw the inflamed Jordanian men fighting the Iraqi soldiers with their bare hands when they spotted the Iraqis pestering their women. Iraqi soldiers used their knives, belts, and pistols against the furious Jordanians. The Jordanians almost always lost in these clashes with the armed Iraqis.

Whenever I saw a Jordanian man stabbed or shot by an Iraqi, a war raged inside me. Part of me wanted to side with the poor Jordanians, and the other didn't want to interfere. I was born in Jordan, and I believed that part of me belonged to the Jordanians even though I was of Lebanese descent.

I often pointed my rifle secretly toward the Iraqis while they fought with the Jordanians, but I could not fire. Our leaders directed us to stay out of the disputes between the Jordanians and the Iraqis. After all, the Iraqis usually hid inside their tanks or fled when our Palestinian militia organizations clashed with each other, no matter how deadly our fighting became. Our leaders used to tell us that the Iraqis were the Jordanians' problem, not ours. They claimed that the PLO didn't need to be involved in any more fighting than they already were.

Besides, my ALF party was allied with the Iraqi government. If I wanted to continue living, my actions had to be neutral. But my thoughts were not. I hated the Iraqis as much as the Israelis, perhaps even more. One moment, in particular, made that rage unquenchable.

IT WAS COMMON FOR THE IRAQIS to drive wildly, speeding their heavy equipment vehicles through Mafraq without regard to the danger they caused. At times, they raced their jeeps through the narrow, semi-paved streets of Mafraq, running over sheep and hens. So much livestock was slaughtered that the Jordanians began referring to the Iraqi army as the sheep hunters.

The sheep and hens weren't the only Iraqis' aggressive driving casualties. There would be more on a bloody March 1970 day. It began peacefully enough, with several Jordanian children playing soccer beneath clear blue skies. Green sprouts were showing through, a sign that spring was soon arriving. Suddenly, an Iraqi truck sped by me approaching the Jordanian kids who were engrossed in their soccer game. The truck raced toward them like a blazing arrow. Time seemed to stop when the Iraqi truck passed me and struck one of the young boys. His body was shredded between the truck tires and the pavement. The truck continued, never slowing down.

I panicked when I saw the child's blood and brain next to his smashed head. I became even more terrified when I saw the child's mother moaning and weeping. She kneeled in the middle of the street, facing her dead child's body. Lifting her arms toward the sky as if wanting to touch God, she shouted, "We don't want the Iraqis here! We would rather live with the Israelis than the Iraqis!"

I stood within several feet of the devastated mother with tears, imagining she was my Mama and I was her son. This was the first time I felt that the Iraqi drivers were as dangerous to the Jordanians and me as the Israeli pilots.

X

DESPITE THEIR BOORISHNESS, Abu Salah, Mafraq's first ALF leader, ensured we didn't do anything foolish to provoke the Iraqis. He was a charismatic man who kept our hate channeled against the Israelis. Our leader was in his early forties. His skin was olive-colored, and he had a rippling chest with bulging muscles across his arms. He was tall and solidly built. He always wore his military uniform except when he made public speeches in Mafraq's market. At these times, he wore a black suit. He had never married and never talked about women. He used to say that Palestine was his bride.

Abu Salah always looked severe and angry, as if he were pissed off at life. His eyes were set deeply in their sockets, and he never smiled. The thick black slashes above his eyes and lips that formed his eyebrows and mustache were long and twisted. I only saw his yellowish teeth when he ate sardines. He would eat sardines directly from the can, using the fingers of his right hand while the sardine can rested in his left palm. Sometimes he finished the whole can of greasy sardines with just two bites. We referred to our leader as "the Shark" because of his love for sardines.

Whenever Abu Salah addressed me, I felt as if I were prey, and he could devour me at any time, knowing he had the power to kill me within a matter of seconds. I was careful not to speak with him alone because I was afraid that if by chance I misspoke, he would make hamburger meat of me—a favorite expression of his. I kept my distance from him and never sat in the first row on the ground when he lectured us. I was afraid to respond with anything other than, "Yes, sir, yes, sir."

During my year of service to the ALF, I viewed Abu Salah as the God of Death. He spoke of killing and death all the time. He would say all Israelis, Americans, and traitors should be killed, wishing death for everyone against us. I used to picture the devil's head on his shoulders. The only thing missing was a pair of horns.

Often, I could smell and feel the embodiment of evil in his presence. He always finished his lectures with, "If you want to live longer, do what I say." When he walked, he swung his arms from left to right like a gorilla, and when he talked to his assistant, his voice took on a ferocious, menacing quality. His eyes penetrated like laser rays. I was rarely able to look my commander in the eyes.

Abu Salah had an unpredictable temper. Once, he threw a chair at his assistant during what seemed to be a casual discussion. Another day, while yelling at one of our members, he hit his desk with his bare hand, putting a hole through it. His philosophy was that when he talked, we must all listen and not offer any opinions or suggestions.

Even though I was terrified of my master, I enjoyed listening to his speeches. The Jordanians who owned shops in Mafraq's market considered him one of the most gifted speakers among all the militia leaders in town. He used to lecture us with hot passion about one particular topic. Strangely enough, this wild man of terror and rage would be the vessel to show me that words could be more potent than any burst of anger or even gunfire.

3
DEMOCRACY AND ASSASSINATION

THE HELLFIRE RAGING FROM ABU SALAH was the same as when he roared that all Israelis and Americans must die. And we listened to him as we always did—without a sound, not even to clear our throats.

But the words from Abu Salah were so different— unlike any I'd heard before. He shouted at the top of his lungs that for the Arab people to defeat their ene- mies, they must change their governance. To defeat these devils, the Arabs must adopt a new brand of politics.

Democracy.

"It is the best resource to help our society become alive," Abu Salah cried. "Wherever democracy exists, power will exist."

He made me fall in love with democracy and view it as the goddess of victory, even though I didn't know what it meant. It was the first time I had ever heard of it. I never encountered a single person in Mafraq who mentioned this mysterious concept. Whenever Abu Salah talked about it, he looked decidedly happy, and if he loved it, I did, too. Each time he said "democracy," I clapped and shouted from deep within my lungs, "Democracy, I love you!" The following day, I would go to school and tell my classmates about my love for democracy and how much I revered it, although I didn't know what to say when asked to define it.

Abu Salah's belief in democracy was primarily due to his hatred of monarchy rule. As long as we had kingdoms in the Arab world, he told us, we would never defeat Israel. He hated many of the Arab kings and presidents. The only two Arab presidents Abu Salah respected were Egypt's Gamal Abdel Nasser and Iraq's Ahmad Hassan al-Bakr. Without their financial support, our organization would not have survived. Abu Salah repeatedly told us that most Arab leadership must be replaced by believers in democracy.

Of course, he never uttered a word of direct praise for Israel or the United States. But looking back, I see the obvious. Abu Salah didn't understand the true meaning of democracy. He simply believed it was the antithesis of the autocratic regimes he despised. However, as a preadolescent, Abu Salah was much more than a bloodthirsty warrior. He was part visionary.

Democracy would prove to be my savior. However, it would not be Abu Salah's.

X

IT WAS FEBRUARY 20, 1970. I would turn twelve in a little over a week. Smartly dressed in his black suit and neatly pressed white shirt, Abu Salah stood atop a table as he kept his eyes fixed on the people. The ALF had just staged one of its Friday rallies in the middle of Mafraq's only market, where people bought vegetables, fruits, bread, live chickens, and sheep every day of the week. He always delivered a speech at the conclusion of rallies as onlookers stood outside the shops to listen. His speeches usually went about three hours. This one was to be about democracy.

My hero began by saying that we all had to stand together against the imperialists and the old societies. People shouted: "Yes, yes, that is right! Long live our leader Yasser Arafat, Abu Ammar!" The people then erupted into applause.

Abu Salah then praised Nasser, proclaiming that the Egyptian leader would throw all the Israelis into the Mediterranean. In response, the crowd yelled, "Long life to Gamal, our hero!"

Then, however, he turned to speak about Syrian President Nureddin al-Atassi. My leader had no respect for the government of Atassi because the president supported the Syrian Sahaka Revolution, while the Iraqi government supported my rival militia. The Syrian and Iraqi governments weren't on good terms at the time.

Abu Salah's hands shook as he spoke, and his face became pale. He didn't meet the people's gaze, hiding his face behind the stack of papers he was reading. But his words were loud and clear. He criticized Atassi, claiming the Syrian leader knew nothing about democracy. He then accused Atassi of working for Israel and America, saying there was no room for traitors and cowards.

My leader's words shocked the crowd. Some of the militia listening to the speech started to boo, especially those who belonged to the Sahaka organization. Many others began to walk away from the market. The Jordanians stood frozen in front of their shops. Even my fellow ALF members and I were stunned.

Then Abu Salah said we must take care of the traitors first before facing our enemies in Tel Aviv and Washington. He shouted that during the 1967 Arab-Israeli war, the Syrian army was the first to flee the battle because they were all chickens and traitors.

The Sahaka members erupted. "Go to hell, asshole!" one screamed at Abu Salah. "You are the only traitor here!"

"We are going to kill you! You will pay a high price for that, you motherfucker!" shouted another as most of the Jordanian men started to run inside their shops to hide.

The only ones left in the street listening to Abu Salah were the ALF members, who clapped and cheered nervously. Suddenly, I heard shots coming from behind. Many onlookers ran toward the shops for cover. I ducked to the ground, as did other ALF members. Very few started shooting back in response to this unknown threat. I was scared and confused.

My leader stayed on the table and shouted, "Death to Syria! Death to Nureddin al-Atassi! Death to the Sahaka!"

They were his last words. A shot rang out. A bullet struck my hero in the forehead. Abu Salah collapsed, falling from the table onto his back. He was dead.

The sight of blood pouring like a river from Abu Salah terrified me. Within seconds, there was a pool of it in the street. Moments ago, my leader stood as a hero, his voice resounding like an angry lion's roar, and now he was lying on his back in his blood with a bullet hole in his head.

Shooting and screaming came from every direction. I lay down on my stomach approximately forty feet from Abu Salah. My mouth went dry, and I could not utter a sound. I thought I had lost my voice for good. Coldness spread throughout my body. Suddenly, I forgot how to operate my rifle; it became an unfamiliar appendage. I saw many of the ALF members lying on their stomachs like me. Some stared at the leader's body, and others at the shops, perhaps planning to get up and run there to hide.

I continued looking at my chairman's blood, studying the direction in which it was moving. I did not want Abu Salah's blood to touch my body. I was afraid that I might have an aura of death if it touched me.

Eventually, many men got up from the ground and ran toward the shops, but my legs were too weak to carry me when I tried to get up. I stayed still on my stomach for a few minutes while the shooting echoed. I told myself I was not yet ready to die. Even though watching my chairman die had already slain part of me, I had to live through this.

An older, fatherly man who belonged to my militia group pulled me away from the middle of the street to a grocery shop for safety. His name was Abu Jehad. Propping me against one of its walls, he told me to stay put. He then left and went to stand with the other men next to Abu Salah's body. I didn't know what I was supposed to do—shoot toward the sky like some of the other ALF followers, or cry over the lifeless body of my teacher.

I became more frightened when I noticed some Sahaka members fleeing the scene. Without thinking, I went down on my knees outside the grocery shop where Abu Jehad had pulled me. He came back to me, grabbed one of my arms, and helped me to stand again. "Be brave and tough as you have been taught by the great leader, Abu Salah," he said. "Stop acting like a girl or a cat."

I looked into his eyes, staring at his gray eyebrows and eyelashes, and said, "How do you want me to be tough and brave when you are weak and soft?"

"What do you mean by that?" he asked.

"I saw you crying earlier. You couldn't hide your tears very well," I answered.

Abu Jehad bent down and whispered, "Please don't tell anybody you saw me crying. I don't want the men to think that I am a weak old man." He left again to go into the crowd to stand by the leader's body.

Once I was on my feet, I began to feel dizzy. My vision turned blurry, and I saw hundreds of stars whirling in the blackness of my consciousness.

Abu Salah, whom I was terrified of and respected more than anyone else, was lying on the ground motionless. The man I worshipped was dead under my nose. Conflicting emotions raced through me. I felt guilty. After all, I didn't protect my leader. Angry at the Sahaka militia who had killed my hero, I felt hopeless because I couldn't help. Losing my leader meant I was losing my future. I desperately wished the chairman were standing on the table once again, continuing his speech to clap and cheer for him.

Mafraq had no hospitals or ambulances at that time. Even if it had, it would have been useless as Abu Salah died instantly. The main street emptied quickly now. The shopkeepers and townspeople had run from the market, leaving the open shops behind them. The only fighters left in the market were ALF followers. I decided to go and stand with the rest of them next to my leader's body. Many surrounded the lifeless body of our leader, sheer disbelief on their faces.

I saw tear-stained faces and eyes filled with fear. I felt relieved I was not alone in openly expressing my emotions. I didn't want to be a lesser soldier in the eyes of my fellow members. Our leader had stressed that it was unmanly to show our feelings to anybody. He used to tell us that feelings and emotions were made for weaker beings: women. He said our bodies were made of steel and our blood of a deadly poison more potent than a snake, and our nervous system could withstand any pain. Looking around me now, I realized that most, if not all of us, had at least temporarily dismissed our teacher's lectures.

Six ALF militia members wrapped Abu Salah's body gently with Palestinian flags and, standing three on each side, lifted it onto their shoulders. They sang patriotic songs as they began their mourning march back to headquarters. The rest of us followed closely behind. Soon we all joined in song. Occasionally, we shot a few random bullets into the sky to show respect.

I was walking with the ALF soldiers, my head pointed toward the ground, tears cascading down my face, barely able to lift my shaking feet. I felt like a lost and confused sheep without its shepherd boy to protect and guide it. The man who made me believe we were going to liberate Palestine from the Israelis was now gone for good, killed at the hands of Arabs, not Israelis. My leader who I thought was more substantial than a Mafraq desert storm, more demanding than its rocks, and more powerful than the desert wolves—turned out to be just a man. I kept asking myself how that was possible. I told myself he would come back to life once we arrived at ALF headquarters. I decided to sing with the crowd.

Palestine, the mother of our freedom, one day we will all return to live there again.

Palestine, my beautiful country, my love and my heart belongs to you.

I kept singing the song repeatedly with my fellow soldiers. Our singing was interrupted only when someone occasionally shot his gun toward the sky. As we neared headquarters, I started to think, "How can I live in Palestine again when I never lived there in the first place? How can I love Palestine and give my heart up to it when I didn't know anything about it?"

We were about a block from headquarters, following the winding and narrow streets, and I was still deep in thought about Palestine. My legs continued to tremble uncontrollably when we arrived. There was a partially paved road in front of the building. Across the street lay an expanse of open land that lacked vegetation but was covered with powdery desert sand that blew over our heads. The men laid our leader on the ground near the main entrance of the building and began to remove the flags from his body. His clothes were soaked with fresh blood, his face as yellow as a fallen leaf at the end of autumn. Blood flowed thickly and rapidly through the hole in his forehead. Many of us began shooting into the clear Mafraq sky, expelling our frustrations into the endless void.

My eyes stayed focused on the face of my dead leader as some of his assistants began undressing him.

A voice kept insisting deep within my heart that Abu Salah was still alive.

"My leader is just about ready to get up," I said in a wavering voice, devoid of spirit, to a man next to me.

He looked at me with teary eyes and said, "I only wish."

Once the men undressed Abu Salah completely, I started feeling nauseous. They washed our hero's body gently, pouring water over it with kitchen pans. The blood was thick and seemed suspended. It had a strong odor to it, almost like sardines.

As the reality that my teacher was gone forever began to take hold, I was tempted to move closer and wash my whole body with it instead of trying to avoid his blood. I wanted to be a part of him and have his blood's odor stay with me forever. I had my mind set on becoming Abu Salah the Second when I grew up.

Some stood singing patriot songs while others quietly cried during the washing. Still, others wailed, "Death to the Syrian Sahaka! Death to Israel and America!" Many danced in a large circle around our slain hero and chanted, "Please, Allah, take good care of our commander. Please, Allah, put him in heaven." We celebrated the life of our teacher, who had gone to heaven and proved his courage by standing up to the Sahaka traitors. That evening I felt the anguish that people who had witnessed the death of their Lord Jesus must have felt.

As we celebrated our hero's death, Mafraq's sun disappeared. It sunk, hiding behind the desert sand like a shy little girl. It blazed orange like a well-rounded pumpkin, and the sky was coated in hues of blue and crimson. The colors made me think of my hero's blood. Abu Salah's men moved his body into a military jeep and drove him to Amman. He was gone for good, along with my hope.

The orange sky faded to a darker, deeper shade. February's cold wind attacked, and the desert sand began hitting our faces, invading our eyes. The stars appeared more clearly, watching us from far above. I felt so empty and lonely that I did not want to leave. I wanted to be with the men so I would not think about my horrible day. Abu Salah's death devastated me. I would never hear him lecture again about my favorite but mystifying subject: democracy.

My thoughts were suddenly interrupted as one of the ALF members stood on a chair in the little street and shrieked: "The Syrian Sahaka is responsible for murdering our hero! Revenge is the only solution for us! We must attack and kill them all when they least expect it."

He ordered most of us to go home and rest and come back the next day to make plans for attacking the Sahaka. I was one of the last in that sorrowful crowd to leave. I didn't want to go home. I was terrified to go to bed, surrounded by the silent, thick darkness. I did not want to sleep, afraid to dream about Abu Salah.

I started walking the block to my house. The song of Palestine played in my head: "I want to go back to Palestine to live there again." But I continued wondering to myself, "How could the dream of Palestine be real?

49

Why would a Lebanese boy want to live in Palestine, Jordan, Lebanon, or anywhere? What is so special about life anyway?"

My leaders, teachers, and parents taught me when a person died defending his country, he would go directly to Allah and have a better life than the one we now knew. However, I started thinking, "If that is the case, why was I afraid of death today?"

I began questioning my reasons for wanting to be a soldier and to liberate a land about which I knew nothing. Would I have joined the militia if I were a Jordanian Muslim or living in my own country, Lebanon? Would I have joined if the Jordanian children did not make fun of me for being Lebanese and Christian? Would I have joined the radicals if the Jordanian children didn't shout at me, "Go back to your country; you are a stranger. We don't want you here; you don't belong in our country."

The face of Abu Salah rose before me. I asked him how it felt to be dead.

"Do you have a gun if there are any Israelis in heaven?" I asked. "Are you feeling at home in heaven, or like the stranger I am on Earth?"

I begged him to take me with him since I felt life was meaningless now that he was gone. I didn't realize how attached to him I had become until he left me.

When I finally arrived home, my mother was waiting, scared and upset, in the kitchen. She looked as if she had aged since I last saw her that morning. Her hair looked gray rather than brown, and her face seemed longer, almost the shape of a peanut. She was worried about me after hearing of Abu Salah's death. Crying and shivering, she engulfed me in her arms. She insisted I leave the militia that night. My mother said, "We are Lebanese and have nothing to do with Palestine or Yasser Arafat. If you are killed, I will die right after you. I will follow Surraia's steps. Is that what you want to do to me?"

Pulling away, she put her hands on her hips and studied me. "I will talk to the new leader to dismiss you. I do not understand why the militia needs a twelve-year-old boy like you, Nabil, to be a soldier!"

I was very calm and told her I would take care of that independently. She made me promise to quit the militia.

Later that night, as Mama made me a sandwich of hummus, tomatoes, and olives, she told me that a Palestinian militia group in Amman had killed a Jordanian soldier that morning. She said it was all over the news in the kingdom, adding that this was not the first incident and surely would not be the last. My Mama said she believed strongly that the Jordanian army would eventually clash with the militia and the Iraqi soldiers.

"I do not understand why the Iraqi army is here. Shouldn't they be on the border with Israel instead of here?" she exclaimed. She believed the Iraqis encouraged Palestinians to fight the Jordanian government. I kept lying to Mama that the movement I belonged to was peaceful because I desperately wanted to calm her down. But I knew she was right. I heard rumors at school from some of my Jordanian classmates that the Palestinian militia would revolt against the Jordanian government. I also became more aware of the increased friction between the Iraqi army and the Jordanian people in Mafraq.

Mama asked if I had seen Abu Salah shot. I had to lie so she wouldn't worry about me. I told her I was too far away to see anything. I denied everything. Repeating that I was tired and needed to go to sleep, I avoided telling her the truth. Instead, I scarfed down my sandwich and washed my hands and face in the kitchen sink. I knew the longer I talked to Mama, the more likely she would figure out I was lying. My mother knew me so well she could read me by the look on my face. I did not want her to see my eyes filled with lies and tears. I wanted to hug her forever, put my head on her chest, and let her wipe my tears away after my bloody, deadly day. I wanted to feel her fingers playing with my hair as they did when I was a baby. I wanted to be secure in my Mama's arms, but I knew I could never feel that again. I was not supposed to show vulnerability or emotion to anybody because I wanted to be a good soldier. I wanted Abu Salah to be proud of me even in death.

It was about 10:00 that night when I finally went to bed. I had to be quiet as I went to sleep to not wake up my brother, Muneer, who shared the bed with me. I could hear him snoring, sound asleep. I envied his peaceful night. Lying on my back next to my brother, my eyes remained wide open in the darkness of the tiny room.

The events of the day replayed themselves in my mind like a film. I remembered clapping when my leader attacked the Syrian government during his speech. I remembered waving my arms in the air while carrying my Kalashnikov, jumping up and down, and encouraging him to criticize the Syrian president. I realized that my leader's men and I had egged him on to continue his verbal attack on the Syrians and the Sahaka. We had driven him down the path of his death. I told myself that my clapping and cheering cost him his life.

In the middle of these thoughts, I rose halfway from the bed and shouted, "I killed my leader, I murdered him, I deserve to be killed!"

Muneer jolted from our bed, yelling, "Nabil is going crazy. He is losing his mind, and I am too scared to share this bed with him!"

My family heard the commotion and clamored around our bed. Mama asked me if I was alright. I told them that I'd had a bad dream. I apologized to my Mama and siblings for waking them up and frightening them. Muneer ended up sleeping next to my oldest brother.

I arose early from bed as the morning light filtered through my window. I was anxious to leave the horrible weekend behind. Weekends usually started on Thursday afternoon and ended Friday night in Muslim countries, so the following week began on Saturday. I was happy to return to school even though I had hardly slept the night before. That morning, I stopped at headquarters on my way to school and learned that someone named Abu Ali would be our new leader.

The horror of the previous day gave way to excitement. I couldn't wait for the day to end to meet Abu Ali. I imagined him to be a carbon copy of Abu Salah in both appearance and action, and it gave me hope that my dream still lived on. I wanted the new leader to talk about democracy just like Abu Salah did. I wanted to hear more about ridding the Middle East of the Arab kings and presidents to welcome democracy to our land. I became so enamored of the word "democracy" that it filled my thoughts, becoming a talisman.

When I finished school late in the afternoon, I ran to ALF headquarters to meet my new hero. The building was suffocating and crowded. It took me more than twenty minutes to squeeze through the packed bodies just to get a peek at the new leader, who had been transferred to our office in Mafraq from the high command center in Amman. There were more than fifty men in the leader's office. Everyone stood except Abu Ali, who was sitting on an old chair on top of the only desk in the room. The right rear leg of the chair rested about a foot away from the hole Abu Salah made when his hand slammed into the desk.

I was astonished when I first saw Abu Ali. He wore his military uniform, but he didn't look like our dead leader. He was short and skinny and did not have one defined muscle in his body. He kept smiling at the men around him. Compared to Abu Salah, he looked like a minnow, which was disappointing. I found myself unable to talk to Abu Ali or even shake his hand. Looking more carefully, I couldn't get over how different he looked from Abu Salah. Abu Ali was in his mid-thirties with dark skin, hair, and thick glasses. His hair was short, and he was clean-shaven. When he removed his glasses, his eyes looked as innocent as a baby's. Abu Ali walked with a limp due to a gunshot by an Israeli soldier during the 1967 war.

This new leader was polite and affable. Unlike Abu Salah, he knew how to say "thank you" and "good morning," which made me concerned. I wondered, "How could he survive here with this personality type?" He said he had finished two years of college in Palestine before the war began and was undoubtedly the most educated person we had ever met among the militia parties.

The first thing Abu Ali did when he took his position was to order us to place a black flag next to every Palestinian flag on the headquarters' walls and the roof of the building. The black flags remained for a week as a sign of respect to Abu Salah.

Shortly afterward, he decided we must not participate in rallies in the market street when the Syrian Sahaka held theirs because the Syrian organizations were traitors working for America and Israel. He also said that he wouldn't make as many speeches as Abu Salah. Our primary objective became clear: to fight with Israel and America. Abu Ali emphasized that desert training and self-defense against Israeli warplanes were more critical than rallies. He designated two Fridays out of every month to have small rallies without speeches, and the remaining Fridays would be used for training in the desert.

Abu Ali told us we must not waste our energy fighting other Arab militia groups. When Israel attacked, they did not usually distinguish among the PLO, Sahaka, or ALF. Every drop of blood we wasted by fighting other Arabs would be a significant loss to us and our homeland, Palestine. Our goal was not to kill Arab people but to kill Israelis. He insisted that if the Sahaka, or any other militia organizations, tried to create trouble with us, we should avoid them and walk away peacefully. He even forbade us to shoot at the Sahaka if they began shooting at us. Abu Ali theorized that a man who wins peace among his people is as much of a hero as the man who wins a battle against his enemies.

Most members of our organization disagreed with Abu Ali's theories and philosophies. His ideas were new to me. I had never heard anyone from any militia organizations talk about peace. I thought the new leader was either mentally ill or a traitor. How was he expecting us to walk away from trouble when the Sahaka were the ones who always started the fighting with us? This question resounded in every member's head.

Like Abu Salah, Abu Ali lived in the ALF building. He had a mattress that stood against a wall inside his office that he slept on at night. There was a small frame on his desk with the picture of a young woman and a little girl. The woman wore a long blue dress. It was nearly ankle length. A white shawl covered part of her long, straight black hair. She carried a little girl who looked less than two years old in her right arm. The baby was dressed in a bright red dress and white stockings. Her eyes shone big and bright through the photograph, and a broad smile across her face matched the smile Abu Ali had given his men. Abu Ali often ran his right thumb along the entire length of the photograph's glass while talking from behind his desk.

I was curious about the individuals in the picture, especially after watching Abu Ali stare at them so often, far away. Later, I learned from one of the other members that his wife and little daughter depicted in the photograph were killed during the the1967 war.

Sometimes, while holding the picture frame between his hands, eyes watery, he remarked that training to survive an Israeli air raid was the most important concern. You could never have enough training on surviving skilled Israeli pilots and their bombs. Training in the desert involved a series of intensive courses on target shooting, handling grenades, and firing of antitank rockets from massive Russian-made guns we carried on our shoulders. Russia was the primary country providing Palestinian organizations with weapons, while America was the provider for Israel. The cold war between these two great countries resulted in a hot war between the Palestinians and the Jews.

We trained to jump through a series of burning

tires to prepare for escaping a fiery building hit by an Israeli rocket, and we learned how to find the best places to hide if warplanes attacked. This part of the training invigorated me. I felt that if an Israeli warplane hit our house, I could help my family survive. In my mind, the safety of my family, especially my Mama's, was my responsibility. Although I was the youngest in the family, I felt I could replace Dad while he was gone. During these ever-increasing interludes, I forced myself to fill my father's shoes.

The feeling stayed with me until the following month when my father finally returned to Jordan from Saudi Arabia. Although I had not been close to Baba, I had waited to see him ever since he left us in March 1967. I missed hearing his manly voice in the house.

4
RETURN OF DAD

MY FATHER, KAREEM, was shorter and smaller than my mother. His gray, thinning hair made him appear partially bald. He had a slight belly that protruded over his trousers, and his face was red as blood. He wore brown sandals with a khaki short-sleeved shirt and dark brown pants during the summer season. In the winter, he wore black boots with two pairs of black wool socks, long johns under his dark-colored pants, and dark long-sleeved shirts. Baba never wore suits or ties except at weddings and funerals.

Two weeks after my dad arrived in Mafraq from Arabia, he opened his clinic within the city limits to cure ailing Jordanians. His clinic was three blocks away from our house and had two separate rooms and a bathroom. Baba ran the clinic by himself. Sometimes my siblings and I went there to mop and clean for him. Baba's clinic was always filled with Bedouins who needed medical attention. He usually opened his clinic at seven in the morning and closed at noon for lunch and a nap. Baba reopened his clinic from 2:30 in the afternoon until six in the evening.

He was generally happy except for the times he fought with Mama. Baba and Mama fought frequently and sometimes wouldn't talk to each other for weeks. I hated seeing them arguing and screaming at each other. Mama yelled at Baba for being out all night, every night. He gambled away the money he made from the clinic that day and then came home between two and three. The fighting started early in the morning when Baba returned home. After drinking all night, he would come into the house, slam the door behind him, and wake up the whole family. Mama would shout at him for being drunk, noisy, and inconsiderate.

Many times my siblings and I were pulled into our parents' disputes. My two brothers, Muneer, two years older than me, and Basem, six years older, always backed up Baba. They felt that boys should be on their father's side. My two sisters and I had different notions. Jehan was three years older, and Sonia was seven years older than me. We always sided with Mama. We believed she was always right, and Baba was always wrong. Luckily, Aida, my oldest sister, lived too far away to become involved with these parental entanglements.

My dad never forgave me for taking Mama's side. He told me I should have been a girl to love my Mama and feel closer to her than to him. I needed to learn from my brothers how to be a real boy, he told me; I shouldn't act like a little girl who loved her mommy's attention all the time. He often said that God made a mistake when he created me. Each time Baba made these comments, he hurt me deeply, mainly when he talked this way in front of his patients. He broke me. I despised my dad's criticisms; they made me feel like a lesser boy.

My two older brothers felt the same way toward me as my dad, but that changed. They saw me as a different boy when I started to appear at home in the evening with a Kalashnikov in my hands. However, I again lost their respect when they caught me hugging and kissing Mama in our backyard. They'd taunt me during these inopportune times, saying, "The truth can't be hidden for long; he can't live without his mommy, just like a baby." Their insults made me believe that boys shouldn't show their emotions and love to anybody, not even their Mamas. The more abuse I received from my brothers and Baba, the more walls I built between them and me.

Baba was very friendly to outsiders, utterly different from when at home, almost like he had two personalities. His green eyes had a warm sparkle that lit up his clinic. Mafraq's Bedouins thought the world of my father and believed he was brilliant, a magical man that cured them and their children. They admired Baba's generous and caring ways. Many of them brought the daily newspaper to my father's clinic, as he read them the news and events occurring in the region. Most Bedouins were illiterate.

I felt proud of my Baba for his role in the medical

profession and owning his clinic. He was much more intelligent than most of the men I knew in Mafraq. When my father read the newspaper to the Bedouins, a warm satisfaction grew inside me. I was glad that I was his son in so many different ways but didn't care for his lack of respect for me. Regardless, in the Arab culture, children are brought up to respect their elders, especially their fathers. Family and the tribal concept are paramount.

Most Jordanians envied us for being part of Kareem's family. Jordanian women told Mama she was a lucky woman for being married to Kareem. Mama answered, "You are a lot luckier than I because my husband treats outsiders a lot nicer than he treats his own family." Her comments shocked and upset the Jordanian women. They didn't believe Mama and thought she was ungrateful and rude.

When Baba returned from Saudi Arabia, he brought a small monkey as a present for the family. We all loved her and named her Sana. She was about 10 pounds with large, dark pools for eyes and a bright red butt. When I called her name, she came running and jumped on my lap. She was a great listener, never interrupting me when I talked to her, unlike my siblings. She quickly became part of our family, and I became very attached to her. Our new family member was not only intelligent but wise as well. Sana seemed to read my emotions, sensing if I was sad, worried or happy. She became a good friend of mine, and I loved spending time with her. Feeding her bananas and bread, I sat and talked with her about my days. Most of the time, I thought of Sana more as a human girl than as a monkey. She reminded me otherwise when she made strange guttural noises as I talked to her. Although she loved all my siblings, her heart was with me.

I was the only one in our family who let Sana do as she pleased. My brother Muneer, who shared the bed with me, did not allow her to sleep with us. I often snuck out to sleep with Sana on her blanket under the antique table in our kitchen. I enjoyed hugging her tightly to my little body, smelling her, hearing her breathing, and kissing her on the head. It felt a lot safer to be closer to Sana than to Mama. Spending time with Sana was an emotional escape valve. I needed to love her, hug her, and feel secure lying next to her.

Each day I passed with the militiamen, I imitated their rugged and macho exteriors until I could play with and cuddle my new baby, Sana. Unfortunately, my care-free happiness with that little monkey didn't last very long. My siblings began making fun of me whenever they caught me holding her and telling her I loved her. My parents also reprimanded me, telling me to calm down when I embraced Sana. They didn't want me to sleep with the monkey because she was female. They shouted at me to leave her alone.

They were probably right, but I enjoyed feeling Sana's body against mine. I thought I could feel the love and emotions I directed towards Sana because she wasn't a human being, and I wouldn't be less of a man. But I soon realized that being close to a monkey was also against the unspoken rules of our society. My parents didn't allow me to hug or kiss Sana for more than ten minutes during any twenty-four-hour period. I often cheated, holding her when Mama was busy with household chores and Baba was at his clinic.

I wondered, "Why does love have to be monitored? Why are we allowed to hate our enemies and not allowed to love our family?" Baba had a different theory about my love for Mama and Sana than mine. As the youngest and most sensitive child, I believed that my love for them should have been open and accessible, while my father thought I should be an independent soul with no emotional attachments. My siblings didn't feel they needed outside love; unlike me, my two sisters were allowed to show their love and affection towards Mama, and my two brothers were content with the love and respect they received from Baba.

My dad's differences with me centered on my relationship with Sana and Mama and my membership with the ALF. Shortly after returning from Saudi Arabia, he became furious with me because I joined a Palestinian militia group while he was away. The severe clashes between the Palestinian militia and the Jordanian army in Jordan did not help Baba understand why I joined the militia. He continually advised me to leave the ALF. Never having a close relationship with my father, I did not care to hear his advice. He had deserted us for three long years, and the arguing with Mama made me distant from him, draining any feelings of trust.

As he folded up the Jordanian newspaper he had been reading, my father told me the Palestinian militia planned to make Jordan their new home. "They are not here to liberate Palestine from Israel; they came to take over Jordan from the Jordanians." He handed me the crushed newspaper and told me to use it for wiping ourselves in the bathroom. On my way there, he followed me, yelling, "They are here to transform the Kingdom into a Republican Palestine." I tried to ignore my dad's comments, walking away.

It didn't take me long to realize my dad was right. A few weeks after his return, a rumor circulated that several militia members attempted to assassinate the Jordanian King. My whole family, including me, was shocked. Mama could not stop crying. She liked King Hussein. She referred to him as angel Hussein because she believed he was a peaceful leader. My dad, who had never liked the King, altered his feelings completely. After seeing Mafraq filled with unlawful Palestinian and Iraqi soldiers instead of the disciplined and orderly Jordanians, he became sympathetic towards the King. He told us he was sick of watching the Palestinian militiamen drive Mafraq and its residents to hell with their relentless rallies and battles. He said he'd rather see King Hussein's soldiers here than these gangs.

When militiamen attempted to assassinate the King on that particular day, Baba had come home early from his clinic. He approached me while I was sitting on the floor of the kitchen playing with Sana. Shouting at me, he said he was confident the Palestinians and the Jordanians would begin fighting soon. He insisted I leave the militia. He pointed his index finger toward my face and said, "If you ever raise your gun to a Jordanian face, it would be the same as raising a gun to my own. Jordan and the Jordanians are everything to me. I have been living in this country since 1948, and now it has become part of me. If you are planning to support the militia by fighting the Jordanians, you are fighting me, which means you are not giving me any choice but to disown you."

His tirade shocked me. I didn't want to be disowned by Baba. If he disowned me, I would no longer be able to see my Mama and siblings. Stopping me from seeing Mama meant stopping me from breathing. I knew I couldn't do that.

I could tell Baba was very serious and meant everything he said. If I were disowned, I would have to leave my home and move in with a militiaman. Moving out of the house would draw me away from Sana, too. And I knew Mama and Sana needed me as much as I needed them. My siblings and parents liked Sana, but not nearly the same way I cared for her. I was the one who always made sure Sana had food and water. I was the one who always snuck out in the middle of the night to crawl into her bed under the kitchen table to sleep next to her. I was afraid if I was kicked out of the house, Sana would die of hunger. I wished Baba had stayed in Saudi Arabia. I might not have met my friend Sana, but I wouldn't have faced this ultimatum.

I became confused, trying to puzzle out a solution. Tears streamed down my face trying to wash my pain away. I felt like screaming at Baba and telling him to take a hike or go to hell, but I knew I'd be whipped with the small hose that he always kept hidden in his locked suitcase. Whipping a child with a belt, a hose, or striking him with a stick were the primary forms of discipline in Jordan.

My dad's love for the Jordanians was not a one-sided affair. They loved him back. He was the only person working in the medical field in Mafraq from 1955 to 1965. Some Bedouins who lived in Mafraq and the surrounding area called him "Nabey," meaning "prophet," because he cured them of their illnesses. Although he was born and raised in Lebanon, he considered Jordan his home. Baba lived in Mafraq from the year he secured his first job, 1948, until he passed away in 1995. He requested burial in Mafraq amongst the Jordanians who were everything to him, not in Lebanon, his homeland.

Despite all the arguments I had with Baba regarding my status in the militia, part of me knew he was right, although I continued my involvement with the ALF organization. I attended their rallies and joined them in desert training exercises. Six weeks after Baba returned to Mafraq from Arabia, his anger peaked. He told me if I did not leave the ALF by June 1, I would be kicked out of the house. He said he was as serious as the Kalashnikov I owned. If I didn't quit the militia, Baba told me he would go to ALF headquarters and ask them to find a place for me to live or release me entirely from their organization.

My dad's threats devastated me. I didn't want Baba to talk to Abu Ali. I was afraid that one of the militiamen might maim or shoot him and my entire family. I couldn't continue living if I were the reason for Baba's death or any family member's. At that moment, I knew I had to resign from the ALF before the first day of June, as that day, we were planning to leave Jordan for Lebanon for the summer break.

Another reason for leaving the ALF came on the first Friday of May 1970, when I was in the desert with fifty other members of the ALF training squad. Abu Ahmad, the training leader, was assigned by the slain leading commander, Abu Salah. He was in his thirties, tall, with a protruding belly and a front tooth missing. His head was hairless, and he never smiled. Abu Ahmad yelled at me because I was not concentrating on shooting at the target. He told me in no uncertain terms that he would have to impart punishment if I did not improve. Punishment in the militia groups came in different colors: red if the leader used his knife, blue and purple if he used wooden planks.

Abu Ahmad terrified me. I did not want to bear his wrath, so I promised to improve my target shooting. He made me shoot again, and I missed the target once more.

He delivered a stinging slap to my face and ordered me to crawl on my stomach for a few minutes. The dust and sand of the desert clogged my mouth and nose, and I gagged so hard I couldn't breathe. After finishing my penance, Abu Ahmad returned to me and put his pistol against my head. He told me to improve my shooting or the Front would no longer need me. I froze as his gun touched my skull. I shivered and told him I was ill and would do better next time. Abu Ahmad thrust his pistol back into his pants behind his belt buckle and walked away. Terrified and confused for the rest of the day, I counted each minute until I could go home and feel secure again with Mama and Sana.

When the day finally ended, I ran to my house. I was relieved to arrive alive but kept thinking about Abu Ahmad with his cold pistol leveled at my head. I was shaken but could not open up to my mother, who I feared would lose her mind. My dad spent most of his time at his clinic or with his Jordanian friends playing poker and drinking arak, a Lebanese brew that tasted like ouzo and was rich in alcohol. I hoped time would stop and did not want the following Friday to arrive.

I kept telling myself that this bastard was either trying to humiliate or kill me. I thought about complaining to Abu Ali but then remembered my friend Salem, who complained about Abu Ahmad. The day after complaining, Salem was beaten up by Abu Ahmad. For several weeks, his injuries transformed him to look like a monster. Sadness and fear dogged me the entire week. I felt sad for my Mama, who would go insane if I were shot, and scared of the unknown punishment that Abu Ahmad had planned for me.

Friday morning eventually arrived. I hugged each family member fiercely, especially my mother before I left. I thought deep inside that I would never see them again. Feeling such a sense of heavy sadness, I could not bear to tell them what might happen during training that day. The only one I told was Sana. I told her to take care of Mama after my death. I confided in Sana that Mama was right from the beginning; I shouldn't have joined these gangs. I left the house with tears stored away behind my eyes.

I met some of the ALF members at headquarters, and we all jogged to our designated place in the desert where Abu Ahmad usually stood next to his jeep waiting for us. We noticed that neither Abu Ahmad nor his familiar green jeep was there upon arrival. I was ecstatic that he had not shown up. He never missed any activity with our group, which filled me with wonder and gratitude.

We stood around in the same spot where the green jeep should have been parked and waited for Abu Ahmad. Fifteen minutes passed when another jeep pulled up. Inside rode a young man in his twenties named Abu Ghadab. Abu Ghadab had light brown curly hair and olive-colored skin. He was almost six feet tall and slim, his body bent in the shape of an olive tree branch. I knew Abu Ghadab well. Last month, he brought his father, who had asthma, to my father's clinic for medical attention. Abu Ghadab recognized me right away, and we exchanged a couple of smiles.

Abu Ghadab asked us to stand in three separate lines and paced before us, looking anxious. He put both his hands behind his back and told us he would be the new leader of our training group from now on. Abu Ahmad and two other members of our group had been transferred to Amman the day before. Everyone in the training camp was surprised. Many of the ALF soldiers said they were going to miss Abu Ahmad. I was never going to miss him.

Unlike Abu Ahmad, Abu Ghadab was calm and didn't threaten or punish anyone during training. During the daylong session, he concentrated on surviving an air raid instead of shooting. We had all been trained to survive an airstrike, but he insisted that we needed more intensive training. Abu Ghadab, like Abu Ali, said that many people were killed during Israeli warplane raids because they did not know how or where to hide during the strikes. He said that the number one killer was shrapnel, not bombs, during such attacks. We would all die during an Israeli raid unless we learned how to hide and avoid shrapnel. His words took me back to three years earlier, and I started thinking about my little friends, Maneh and Amjad.

It was back in June 1967, when I was nine years old. Maneh, Amjad, several other children, and I decided to meet at the schoolyard to play soccer, as we usually did each afternoon. The school was out for the summer, and most of the children I played soccer with were classmates. About twenty children played regularly, and because Maneh and Amjad were my favorite friends, we always managed to be on the same team.

The three of us first met when we were four years old. We shared both laughter and tears in school. The first year in kindergarten, we sat next to each other, although we hardly sat still. Later in the third grade, one day, we started laughing while the nun lectured us in math. I don't remember the reason for our burst of laughter, but I remember when two nuns took off our shoes and had each of us put our knees on the seat of a chair, our stomachs facing the back of the chair. The nuns tied a rope around our waists to the back of the chairs and whipped the underside of our feet with a coarse belt. We were all in pain for days.

Maneh and Amjad were neighbors. Their houses were located close to the town market. They always walked home together after school, and I envied them. My house was located on the other end of the village, which meant we seldom saw each other after school. When we did, we enjoyed each other's company immensely. I especially appreciated studying math with Maneh because he was brilliant. He understood our fourth-grade math book as though he were the author. Sometimes, he dared to correct the nun who taught the class, and we called him the father of math. Although he was much more intelligent than anybody else in the class, he never bragged. He never pretended he was better than the rest of us and helped everyone with math homework.

I also liked studying Arab history with Amjad. He knew everything about the Arabs' past. It was as if he had lived for centuries. He even memorized a couple of books on Arabic history. We used to call him "Grandpa" for this reason. Amjad was also great at sports and an energetic child who never seemed to tire of athletic activity or talk. Both Maneh and Amjad were skilled soccer players, but Amjad was the fastest runner.

Though it was a hot day for soccer, we decided to play anyway. The sky was a perfect summer canvas: clear, blue, and without clouds.

The soccer game had just started, and we were all having a good time running and chasing the ball, shouting at each other, and trying to be the first team to score. It was early afternoon; the school grounds were deserted except for us. We felt like we owned the school playground. Maneh had the loudest voice on the field. He was always anxious to win a game and did not hesitate to express this desire. He shouted at the other team, telling them he would defeat them. He told them to get out of his way or he would knock them to the ground. I was so hot that the sweat drenched my clothes, although I was not pushing as hard to score as Amjad and Maneh. I was not the natural athlete that my two friends were.

Amjad was very close to scoring a goal when suddenly, we heard a massive explosion coming from the desert where a Jordanian military airport was located. We stopped playing. We exchanged terrified looks. Another blast followed, this one louder and closer. I felt faint; maybe the world was coming to an end. Two more explosions ripped through the desert until we heard blasts coming from all around us. It seemed there was smoke emanating from Mafraq's only market, turning the sky from pure blue to sooty black. I was so shaken; I did not know what to do. I thought this must be a nightmare.

All the children ran from the playground except me. I stood still by myself in a panic. My underwear became saturated as I tried to figure out where to go and what to do. All the children had disappeared. There seemed to be no way out of this hell, and I had forgotten where my house stood. Smoke columns continued to climb in the sky; the explosions came more quickly, one after the other, suddenly closer and louder each time. My mind was a blank, filled with confusion and terror. I felt death was all around, bearing down on me, when I saw flames shooting out from the military airport.

Still, I knew I had to move. I began running in the direction of the Latin Church, which was part of the school and located adjacent to it. Rushing into a corner between two massive church walls, I looked skyward, searching for help. Israeli planes screamed all over Mafraq. They bombed mercilessly with hardly any resistance from the Jordanian army that had focused its efforts at the border of Israel.

The planes looked like giant ferocious birds, flying

in random and strange patterns. The sunlight broke through the veils of gray and black every few minutes, and the dazzlingly bright light hurt my eyes. My vision became blurred, even as I realized that bombs were falling from the planes. The bombs looked like giant marbles, pieces of a child's game. Sometimes the planes flew high; other times, they soared so low I thought they would land on my head. The exploding bombs and screeching planes made a symphony louder than thunder. The church windows shattered, and some of the glass fell to the ground a few feet from me.

I prayed to see somebody. Though I had only taken shelter for a few minutes, I felt as if I had been there for days. My whole body shook with each violent blast, and the tears streamed down my face. I felt my end was near. I started talking to God, asking him why this was happening. I begged him to take these planes away. I finally told him I was not yet ready to meet him.

"Please let me live," I shouted.

The bombing was relentless, and the explosions continued to echo all around me. My heart and lungs burned; I had to sit down on the ground. Folding my knees up to my chest, I hugged them and rested my head on my arms. I sat still for a few minutes with the company of my tears. My body continued to jerk. A sharp pain settled into my neck until I thought I would never straighten it.

Some time elapsed, and I started to feel secure between the two large walls. I surrendered to reality and had given up my fear. A peace grew inside me and the bombs and the planes became my favorite musical song. I remember closing my fingers tightly into each palm, hiding my life within them. My tears refused to drop anymore, and my knees stopped shaking. Thoughts of death and thoughts of my mother filled my mind. As my mind turned increasingly to Mama, I decided to survive that hellish raid. I imagined my mother kneeling above my coffin with tears covering her face. My dad was in Arabia, oblivious to what was happening here. I knew Mama was probably sick with worry over me, and I should run home to let her see me alive again.

I finally managed to compose myself and figured out the way home. I started to run like a deer. I had never run that fast before. This energy was born of fear and a desire to live, to see my Mama's face again. The street was barren except for a donkey standing next to a house. I felt sorry for it, but I could not stop; my legs were moving out of control. My arms pumped back and forth like a machine. I kept my eyes straight ahead, not daring to look for the planes. The sound of the bombs continued to scare me, but I kept struggling forward, wishing death to the Israeli pilots above me.

I finally made it to our block, which looked utterly deserted. There was no sign of human life. I was only a few yards away from my home when my heart dropped to my feet. I could not run anymore, so I continued walking in the direction of the main door of our home. The house was very still. I was frightened and disoriented; I wondered what had happened to my family. I felt sure they were all dead. I shouted out to my family and heard my Mama and siblings calling back to me. Their voices came from the bathroom. I ran through the house to be with them. They had been hiding in the bathroom throughout the raid. My mom thought it was the safest place because it did not have windows.

My two older brothers looked panic-stricken and were holding hands. The faces of my two older sisters were ashen as if they had just come back from the dead. They held each other tightly. My poor mother's face looked unfamiliar to me. Her eyes were red from crying, and her face looked pale. She looked as if she had lost the natural smile from her face. She had one arm around the boys and the other around the girls. Mama was overcome with relief when she saw me. I stood in front of my mother, my back next to her, my left arm around the waist of one of my sisters, and my right arm around one of my brothers. The bathroom was tiny, but we stayed in our human knot until the raid ended in midafternoon. Though it lasted for around one interminably long hour, it felt as if it had lasted for weeks. We all thought we'd find the neighborhood in ruins when we stepped out.

When we finally left the house, we went out slowly, forming a straight line with my mother as the lead and me in the rear. There were people outside surveying the whole block, which made me feel more confident about the fate of our neighborhood. Smoke continued to rise in the direction of the desert and the market. There was no damage to our block. The neighbors gathered together outside their homes. They formed two large circles: one made up of men and the other of women. Jordanian Muslim culture at that time dictated that men and women did not mix, not even during air raids. The concept of dating did not exist. People married through arranged marital agreements. If a woman talked to a man alone before marriage or a man who was not her husband after marriage, she was considered cheap.

Many of the neighbors talked politics, each sounding like an expert in the area. People stood outside their homes conversing about the horrors and implications of the war for several hours. At times, a conversation was interrupted by the terrified screams of a child, likely remembering the raid that had raged on only hours ago. Mama and I exchanged looks as the scene continued to unfold. My feelings were muddled; I wished I were standing next to Mama, yet I felt grown-up and masculine standing with the men, and I appreciated the sentiment.

It was early evening when we saw a large group of young men approach our neighborhood. They walked quickly and shouted, "With our soul, with our blood, we will protect King Hussein. This was a lesson to the Israelis that they will never forget!" The young guys closed in on the circle of men and displayed the severed limb of a man. They told us, the arm belonged to an Israeli pilot whose plane had been shot down by the Jordanian army. There was a watch on the arm like I had never seen before. The young men tossed the dead man's arm between them, playing a school boy's game of catch. Sometimes they purposely dropped it on the ground, laughing at it when it fell.

One of my neighbors asked the young men about the rest of the body. They said all they found was an arm. Another neighbor said, a few hours ago, our lives were in the hands of this bastard, and now his whole arm is in our hands. I thought, how many bombs did this arm fire at us? I remained silent, locked inside myself, and thought the whole day had to be a nightmare. The horror that gripped me from the day's events permeated every inch of my body.

The day finally closed, and it was time for us to get some much-needed sleep. I was thirsty for a cup of water, but the warplanes damaged the water storage tank of Mafraq. We had no water in the house. When I was a child in Jordan, we had to drink water, coffee, and tea. Soda and juices hardly existed in Mafraq. My mother told me to say a prayer and to try to sleep.

It was a quiet night compared to the terror-filled day. Afraid to close my eyes, I didn't want to miss anything overnight. I ended up staring at the darkness. I saw myself between the two giant walls of the church and kept thinking about the pilot's arm and his mother. I could not imagine what his mom would do when she heard that her son's plane was shot down. I held myself, trying not to cry and wake up my siblings.

5
SHATTERED SOUL

THE MEMORIES OF MY CLASSMATES, Amjad and Maneh, continued as our militia group took a break from desert training with Abu Ghadab. The following morning after that horrific day, I remembered the Israeli warplanes paying us another visit. My family and I jumped out of our beds and ran to the bathroom. The bombs and explosions were so loud the windows of our home shook as if there were an earthquake. My mother's face turned white. I thought she would faint. We huddled together and shivered like we were buried in a snow bank. The power went off a few minutes later, shrouding us in darkness. I could not read Mama's facial expressions anymore, but she said we should all move to Lebanon. She told us Lebanon was a peaceful country, and it never participated in this war. Therefore, we should not continue to live in Jordan, especially while my dad was working in Saudi Arabia. No one responded. My mouth went dry like the desert.

The bomb drops lasted for a few minutes, but it felt like hours. Eventually, we moved to Mama's room, where we sat on her bed in the dark, waiting desperately for the sun to shine again.

There was some relief when morning arrived. We were all happy we survived the air raid for a second day. My mom kept assuring us that everything would be alright while making us breakfast. Shortly after we finished our meal, we were startled by people talking loudly in the street. My brother, Basem, went outside and a few minutes later, his face ashen, told us he heard that Maneh and Amjad were killed by shrapnel on their way home from the school playground. My soul sank into a deep depression. I was angry at Allah. I told him I was never going to trust him again. I hated myself for playing soccer that day. I felt guilty and told myself I should have made them stay with me or run with them. I became quiet, sad, and isolated from my family, neighbors, and friends. The nights became endless, wracked with pain. I stopped thinking of the Israeli pilot's mother and instead thought of the mothers of my dead friends. Mama caught me talking to myself and crying in our backyard on several occasions. She would come and sit next to me, comforting me and crying. She was very kind, even though she couldn't take away my pain and disappointment in Allah. I cried myself to sleep almost every night for weeks. I couldn't understand why my friends had to go to Allah; I did not know what death meant. Mama tried to explain to me, but I insisted that

Maneh and Amjad would come back to play soccer with me again. I carried guilt and blame for a long time.

Abu Ghadab's voice broke my daydream about Maneh and Amjad when he loudly called my name, ordering me to jump over a burning tire. I skillfully performed this exercise. We put a burning tire on the ground in these drills, positioning ourselves about twenty feet away. Running towards it as fast as possible, we'd jump over the tire, trying not to let the flames catch on our clothes or shoes. After these exercises, we were trained to escape airstrikes alive. We dug in the desert the rest of the day and filled bags with sand as bunkers in Mafraq's streets. The day was long; the work and training stretched on forever. The sandbags were too heavy for a twelve-year-old boy to load onto a truck. Sometimes my palms bled from the work. The new leader was kind enough to let us have a break every two hours instead of four hours as Abu Ahmed had allowed. Remembering my little friends, Maneh and Amjad, cast a shadow on the rest of the day until late afternoon when Abu Ghadab dismissed us.

When I arrived home in the evening, my mother looked ill. As I approached her, I realized she was crying. "What is the matter, Mama?" I asked.

In a weak voice, she said she was disappointed in me. "You promised me back in February, Nabil, when Abu Salah was killed, that you were going to resign from the Palestinian militia. Do you know that the Jordanian army has been battling the militia in Zarqa for the last two hours?" Zarqa was a town in Jordan about thirty miles south of Mafraq. Mama continued, "Can you assure me that Mafraq will not be next?"

"What happened, Mom? Why did the fighting start?" I asked.

"The militias are trying to take over Jordan, Nabil. The Palestinians are planning to make Jordan their new homeland. I beg you to leave these crazy guerrillas. They are up to no good."

I did not respond, but I knew my mother was right. I couldn't tell Mama that staying with the ALF was much safer for the whole family than leaving the organization.

The last thing I wanted to do was point my gun and throw grenades at the Jordanians. I did not enroll with the militia to fight King Hussein's government or the Jordanians.

Mama interrupted my thoughts when she asked me, "Do you think that if Maneh and Amjad were still alive, they would be proud of you if you started fighting the Jordanians? Do you think they would appreciate you shooting at their families, relatives, neighbors, and friends?"

Her questions struck me deep in the heart. Tears were the only answers I could find. My mother watched me cry and seemed to read the pain within me.

"I am sorry I had to say that to you, my baby, but this is the truth. I believe that Maneh and Amjad are watching the militia's aggression from heaven, and I do not think they like what they see."

Confused and scared, I did not know what to do. I thought deeply, remembering the conversation I had heard only a few days before between Abu Sakher and Abu Hasef, the two assistants of Abu Ali. Abu Hasef asked Abu Sakher if he thought King Hussein was an agent of Israel and America. To my surprise, Abu Sakher stated that all Arab leaders were traitors except for Gamal Abdel Nasser, the Egyptian President, and Yasser Arafat. At the end of their conversation, I remembered Abu Hasef saying we would teach all traitors a lesson. They all deserve to be slaughtered, he had said. At the time, I did not take what I heard seriously, but after talking to Mama, I realized the militia organizations might start fighting against the Jordanians one day.

I decided to sleep to escape my thoughts, but I could not. My mind raced over the idea that if King Hussein were a traitor, why did he send his army to fight the Israelis and defend the Palestinians back in 1967? I recalled seeing the King's picture a couple of times on the front page of Jordanian newspapers. They photographed him in a Jordanian military airplane chasing Israeli planes. How could Abu Sakher and Abu Hasef accuse the Jordanian government of being traitors when so many Jordanian soldiers were killed in less than a week back in 1967 while defending Palestinians from the Israelis? I was awake most of the night, thinking about the King, his government, and his army, which I believed was more decent and organized than the PLO organizations.

I also thought about the King's people, whom my dad loved and trusted. I asked myself how I could ever have dared to become anti-Jordanian when I was born in Jordan and grew up there. I wondered what had happened to Nabil, the innocent boy I once knew. Why had the militia suddenly targeted their hostility towards the Jordanians rather than the Israelis? I overheard my Mama talking to the neighbors that there was no reasonable explanation for the bizarre behavior the militia had displayed lately towards the Jordanians. And my Baba's comments about disowning me if I did not leave the ALF kept ringing in my ears. I started to think more seriously about making up an innocuous excuse that would allow me to resign from the militia without arousing suspicion.

Morning arrived, and it was time for me to get up and prepare for school. I went to school as usual, but all I played over and over in my mind was leaving the militia. Much of the day was spent finding a reasonable excuse to give Abu Ali. I was terrified the militia might shoot my family or me dead if I decided to leave. I began to pray an Iraqi Army vehicle would run me over, injuring me, ensuring my departure from the guerrilla group. The plan to throw myself in front of a speeding Iraqi military jeep on my way home from school became my only hope. I told myself all I had to do was stand in the middle of the street, and it wouldn't be long before an Iraqi jeep came careening down the road towards me. I reminded myself to stand where the jeep's side would hit me rather than its front; I was sure to survive.

The time finally arrived in midafternoon for school to end. It was the first time I felt the school day had ended far too fast. I stared at the yellow walls of my classroom and the picture of the King that hung on the front wall facing the students. I looked at each student's face trying to memorize individual facial structures and complexions. I looked at my Arabic teacher, Mr. Mazen, and smiled slyly. Mr. Mazen, tall and handsome, was a friendly teacher. His light brown hair and green eyes made him look quite distinguished. He hardly ever became upset, even when we didn't do our homework. My teacher looked back at me with wondering eyes. He seemed to sense that I was up to something. Before he discovered my plans, I had to drag my eyes away from him. While walking out of the school building, my eyes roamed over the room's white ceiling, filled with many holes. These holes were there because the building was getting old, and nobody ever maintained it.

Once outside, I made sure to walk in the middle of the street, searching for an Iraqi jeep to throw myself in front of. I was almost halfway home and practically in front of the entrance to the ALF headquarters when I spotted an Iraqi truck coming my way. I told myself that this was my lucky moment. I would be free from the militia; they would dismiss me peacefully due to my injuries and not hurt my family or me. The truck moved swiftly towards me, and my legs felt like they were dancing even as they remained still. I stared at the truck as it approached me, coming so close I could see the Iraqi military hat on the driver's head. The driver's horn blared, but I stood still facing the truck, ready to be struck. The truck closed in a few feet away when I leaped to the side of the road, barely avoiding it before it tore me to pieces. I couldn't do this to Mama, I told myself a split second before the truck was upon me. What if I were killed by this truck? Mama would have killed herself. I resumed my walk home, thinking of other alternatives which would allow me to resign from the ALF without wasting a single drop of my blood.

The minute I entered our home, Mama asked if I had resigned from the militia yet. I was just about to tell her that I had been ready to quit life altogether, but I couldn't. I didn't want to worry and upset her. She had enough worries about me and enough anger towards my Baba to last a lifetime. I told Mama, who was aware of Baba's ultimatum, that I planned to leave the militia on May 31, the day before we would travel home to Lebanon for the summer break.

During those twelve days, my Baba reminded me every morning before I left for school that I would be resigning on May thirty-first. He said if I altered my decision about leaving the PLO organization, I would have to move out of the house on June first, and would be forbidden to go to Lebanon with my family. Baba's voice got thicker and louder each morning when he reiterated my resignation date. His resounding statements fell like small bombs. Baba added other layers of pressure on me, more than I could handle. It was hard enough to think about the resignation day, myself, but drilling it into my head repeatedly didn't help. It seemed like he was getting great joy from hearing himself talk about it. Even though I was excited about leaving the ALF, I knew, deep inside, I would miss the members and leaders. None of them ever called me a little girl like my Baba and brothers did. The members had a high level of respect for me; they thought of me as a big tough boy, a martyr, a warrior, and a patriot.

The last week of May was difficult for me. My future was uncertain, and I was afraid of what might happen to my family or me when I told Abu Ali I wanted out of his organization. I felt depressed and empty. I could not continue to be a member of my family as long as I was a member of the ALF, and I was sure I didn't want to give up my family. The only choice I had was to leave this gang.

On the second to last day of May 1970, Baba came home early that evening. He was there before seven and was sober, which was unusual. He carried two brown bags in his arms. Inside one of the bags were two dead hens he handed to Mama, telling her to make dinner. He gave the other bag, which carried potatoes, to one of my sisters and told her to wash them and help Mama. While Mama briskly removed the feathers from the dead chicken's skin, my sisters washed the potatoes in the kitchen sink. Baba opened the closet next to the antique table that Sana slept under and grabbed an empty clear glass. He went to his bedroom, bringing out a bottle of arak. Filling his glass with it, he looked in the direction of my Mama, sisters, and brothers, who watched Mama fighting with the feathers of the chickens and said, "I need to talk to Nabil alone in the backyard, and I don't want anyone to disturb us until I am finished."

I became nervous. I could tell I was in some sort of trouble. I looked at the hand that didn't have the alcohol to see if Baba had his whipping hose. I was relieved to see his empty hand. I thought I had lucked out and he would use the belt around his waist this time. Belt whippings weren't as painful as hose whippings; the marks only stayed for a few days. Hoses left marks that lasted for weeks.

Baba ordered me to follow him to the backyard. I walked behind Baba, following his steps closely. He led me to the olive tree that grew at the end of our backyard. My dad stood under the tree, and I stood facing him a couple of feet away. He looked me straight in the eyes; I became increasingly uncomfortable. I mentally ran down the list of what he might criticize me for: my close relationship with Sana, my excessive love for Mama, or being an ALF member. Baba fixed his eyes on me as if to penetrate my soul. I told myself as long as he didn't reach for his belt, I could withstand this.

Not breaking his gaze, he lifted his right hand that

carried the glass of arak and brought it up between his lips, shutting both lips around the glass's edge and taking a big swig of that potent alcoholic mixture. He took in almost a quarter of the glass in one swallow. He put his hand down, still holding the glass, his eyes still locked on mine, and said: "Nabil!"

"Yes, Baba," I answered cautiously.

He lifted up his right hand, like he was going to swear to tell the truth, placed his glass, again, between his lips, and took another big sip of the clear fluid in the clear glass. By now, the glass was almost empty.

Baba lowered his hand, looked towards the ground, and said, "Nabil, I want to talk with you, man to man." His statement shocked me, almost giving me a heart attack. Baba never referred to me as a man, not even a boy. He always thought of me as a little girl attached to his Mama. He continued. "You amaze me."

"I what, Baba?" I asked him.

He continued looking at the ground, reaching for his mouth with his left hand and wiping his lips of the greasy alcohol. He repeated, "You really amaze me, son."

I looked behind me, thinking he was talking to one of my brothers. There was nothing behind me but olive tree branches. I thought he ought to be drunk; I couldn't believe what he had told me. He had never said anything like this to me before, and I didn't know how to respond to him. I was both thrilled and confused.

Dad took another sip from that glass, finishing the remaining arak. "You know, I can never be what you are.

91

And I am certain that many, many people in this world can't be what you are, but what is amazing to me is that you can be anybody and anything you want. I wish I had half of what you have within your personality. Nabil, can't you see what I am telling you here, son? You have it all. You have it all."

I opened my eyes as wide as I could and asked him, "What do you mean, Baba? What do I have that you wish you had?"

Baba drew a deep breath and said, "I wish I had as much love for my mom. I wish that I could play a tough soldier's role during the day and be a nice son to my mom at night."

I thought I was dreaming, hearing my Baba speak like this. I asked him, "Baba, did you forget how you told me you wished I was as good and manly as my brothers? Don't you remember how often you told people that you only had two sons, Muneer and Basem, and when people asked you what about Nabil, you told them you had no idea how you ended up being my Baba."

Baba said, "I always put you down because I couldn't reach you. You are far away, ahead of and above me. I never thought I would admit this to you in my life, but since tomorrow is your resignation day, I thought it was important for me to share this with you."

"Thank you, Baba, for telling me this. I can't believe it," I told him.

He took a deep breath and asked me, "Did you join the ALF to prove to me that you were a tough boy?"

I looked down and said, "I also wanted to prove that to my siblings and the Mafraq children."

"Well, now you don't need to prove it to anybody; we all know how tough you are," Baba said. He said the only thing I needed to prove was that I was a wise young man and resign from the ALF.

After we all had dinner, I went to bed. My father's words under the olive tree echoed in my mind. I felt happy, excited, and amazed he felt this way. I didn't need to prove to Baba that I was as good as Muneer and Basem anymore. I slept more peacefully that night than I had in a long time.

The following day, I got up excited that this was my last day of school for the year but nervous about my leader's reaction to my resignation. After talking with my dad the night before, I couldn't let him down. I wanted to prove I was a wise young man. I had to leave the PLO organization. If raising a gun towards a Jordanian face signified to Baba that I was raising a gun on his own, I would rather shoot myself. Despite our differences, I still loved and respected him for being my Baba. Respecting parents in the Arab culture is paramount.

Because it was the last day of the year, school ended early. I was home by noon and found Baba home having lunch with Mama. They were happy to see me home early. I told them I would collect all the items belonging to the ALF and return them to headquarters. Both my parents were proud of me.

Baba announced he would be home early that

evening to celebrate my resignation. He and Mama told me that everyone, except Baba and Sana, would be going to Lebanon very early the second morning to spend the summer. We usually went to Lebanon every summer; however, my Baba rarely traveled to his homeland. He loved Jordan and considered it to be his primary home. Mama, in particular, made sure all her children went to Lebanon at least once every two years, if not each year. She wanted to make sure we knew our relatives in the country of our heritage. Besides, my parents owned a beautiful home and several parcels of land in a small village called Ein Eble. Located in southern Lebanon, Ein Eble means "the eye of a baby camel." It stood a few miles from the Israeli border.

It was exciting news to go to Lebanon, but I was sad to leave Sana and Baba behind. I loved Lebanon and my relatives there, especially my third cousin, Laila, two years older than me and a good friend, *Sittie*, my paternal grandmother, and *Jeddie*, my maternal grandfather.

That day, in the early afternoon, I left home to go to ALF headquarters to resign. As I walked there, I thought about the rumor claiming when an Arab shot another Arab, the bullet didn't hurt as much as if it were the bullet of an Israeli. It was a small comfort I clung to. I finally made it to the entrance of the ALF. I walked into the headquarters building, as I had done so many times before, except I did not have bullets encircling my waist. I still carried my Kalashnikov in my right hand, its nose pointed at the ground. The gun was empty of bullets and

I disengaged the bullet cartridge. On my left shoulder, I carried a bag of bullets and boots, and some uniforms that belonged to the organization.

Abu Ali was not there that day. Abu Hasef was in charge. He had fair skin, a black mustache, and a beard halfway down his chest. He looked at me quizzically when I first walked in without the old belt around my waist. He asked instantly, "What is the matter? Why do you look so down?" I informed him immediately, without any warning, that I had decided to leave the militia. He was quite angry by my declaration. His face turned the color of blood. He got up from his chair and put his left foot on it with his leg at a ninety-degree angle. The fingers of his right hand twisted his thick mustache, and his left hand rested on his left knee. With his head slightly cocked as if he were listening for some sound, he stared at my bag of ammunition. I was happy he was not looking straight into my eyes.

He shouted, "Why are you leaving us? I thought in the past you were a young hero. What made you become a chicken all of a sudden?" I did not answer. "So you have made fools out of all of us. You made us think you were part of our organization, and now you are planning to leave us? Do you know what the punishment is for traitors like you?"

He looked directly into my eyes with a fierceness seared into my soul forever.

I dropped my eyes downward and felt my heart race. I started to sweat, the salty discharge stinging my eyes. I did not dare to wipe my eyes. I became as still as a statue. I felt as if the blood had stopped circulating in my body. It occurred to me to run home, but Abu Hasef asked me again in a louder voice this time. "Do you know what the usual punishment is for traitors?" I remained silent. He put his left leg back on the ground and walked toward me. Grabbing my right ear with his left hand, he savagely pulled it. My first impulse was to bite down on his hand, but I controlled myself. I screamed from the pain and lied to him that my mother was waiting outside for me. He stopped instantly. He didn't want Mama to hear my shouting or see him hurting me. Although the militiamen did not mix well with the Jordanian army and its men, they, unlike the Iraqi soldiers, continued to respect the women.

Abu Hasef was shocked when I said Mama was outside. He told me I was like a little girl to bring my mom with me. He said he was not surprised I was quitting because I was Lebanese. He said, "All Lebanese are weaklings and traitors. Your country is the only Arab state that did not fight Israel during the 1967 war. Do you know why your people did not enter the war? Because you are all women. There is not a man in existence in Lebanon!" he shouted. He screamed at me that I had proved I was a traitor, a coward, and a little girl, not a young man, by having my Mama wait outside for me.

I walked shakily towards the door, and once out the door, I ran home as fast as I could. I sped away like a deer running for my life once again. However, I was running away from the Palestinians and not the Israelis.

I entered the house out of breath; my whole family was thrilled I had left the militia. However, we were all concerned about the ALF's reaction to my resignation. My dad informed us that his friend, Mr. Musa, would drive us to Beirut at three o'clock in the morning. My dad never drove or owned a car in his life. My parents thought I shouldn't step outside the house until Mr. Musa showed up in the early morning to go to Lebanon. That way, none of the militia members would see me outside.

I was sad to go to Lebanon without Baba and Sana for the summer. I kept thinking about them the whole late afternoon as Sana sat on my lap or curled up next to me while Mama packed the suitcases with our clothes. I felt Sana knew we were going on a big trip and leaving her behind. That day, my parents dropped their restrictions about holding and kissing Sana, which made me free with my little monkey and allowed me to see her differently. It was a feeling I had never imagined was inside me. It was a new feeling of love and inspiration and a light filled with pure sensation and passion. It happened when Sana and I climbed the olive tree in our backyard that early evening. We neared the top and settled on one of its branches. We were all alone, isolated from everyone, entirely covered by a thick blanket of olive tree leaves. I reached out to Sana and held her tight to my chest as I told her how sorry I was for not taking her with us to Lebanon. I explained that my parents assured me she wouldn't be able to enter Lebanon without special papers needed from the Jordanian government. I told her that Mama and Baba said it would be too difficult for them to get these documents. I kissed her face over and over. She moved to settle on my lap but started jumping up and down, leaving a strange feeling in my crotch. I had never had this feeling before, and it made me feel good but dizzy and confused. I grabbed Sana and held her still to make her stop. I looked down at my crotch and was shocked to see it swollen, almost bursting out of my pants.

I immediately decided to climb down the tree; I didn't know what was happening inside my pants. I decided to tell Mama about what had happened. Mama was upset and slapped me hard across the face. I didn't know what I had done. I ran from Mama out into the backyard. Some moments later, Mama came after me with a belt and whipped my ass until my face was awash with painful tears. I was forbidden to touch or talk to Sana for the rest of the night.

Mama was kind not to tell Baba about my experience with Sana. I made up with Mama a couple of hours after she punished me for having an aggressive crotch. Discussions about sex between children and parents, or teachers, in Mafraq, were wholly forbidden. I hugged Sana and asked her to forgive me for my shameful behavior. I promised my Mama that my crotch would never get swollen as long as I lived. She was good-hearted to accept my apology and trusted my promise.

After I made up with Mama, she allowed me to sit next to Sana under the kitchen table but not put her on my lap again. I apologized to Sana for the aggressive organ hidden inside my pants. I told her she must have been brought up by a more advanced society than ours. I said she was lucky she didn't have to be punished and didn't come from a strict culture like mine. I told her I was the bad guy who felt pleasure from her jumping in my lap. I also explained I was the dumb one who decided to talk to his Mama about this experience. I told my sweet monkey I would be looking forward to seeing her when we returned to Jordan at the end of August. I think she understood what I said, as she made a rasping noise right after I spoke to her.

6
MURDER OF SANA BY MILITIA

AROUND 2:00 AM ON JUNE FIRST, 1970, Mama woke us up to get ready to leave for southern Lebanon. Baba continued sleeping as we left, since he wasn't coming with us. This was not unusual, as he was not sentimental and rarely showed emotion to his family. I did feel empty over Sana not joining us, as she was my second-best friend after Mama.

By 3:00 AM, Mama, my siblings, and I were inside Mr. Musa's car. It was a treat for me to ride in his car. Privately owned automobiles were rare entities in Mafraq at that time.

Once we arrived at the Syrian border, soldiers ordered us to step out of the car. They were rude to us, treating us like animals. They opened all our suitcases and dumped their contents onto the ground, looking for guns or anything of value. They searched us individually in the middle of the street. Taking my mother's purse, they turned it upside down, dropping everything onto the pavement. They ordered my mom on the ground to pick up her precious possessions. Although livid, I was powerless to react.

At around eight o'clock, still waiting for permission to cross the border, we noticed a young Syrian soldier approaching our car. He stopped about ten feet from the car and stared at us. He wore a khaki military uniform, and an automatic machine gun hung over his right shoulder. His black shoes shone like the sun, but he kept surveying us cautiously. I was uncomfortable with the way he looked at my sisters and mother. I tried to intimidate him with my looks. I held my gaze steady, thinking, why are these soldiers keeping us in this heat in this little car? Are they planning to watch us cook to have us for a meal later?

My sister Sonia interrupted my thoughts when she suddenly jumped out of the car, screaming, "A bee! A bee is inside the car!" We scrambled to get out of the vehicle. The soldier who had been scrutinizing us ordered us to reenter the car. The driver told the soldier that a bee was inside the vehicle, and we were afraid of being stung. The soldier looked at the driver, saying, "What do you want me to do? Shoot it? I order you to stay inside your car, or I'll have you all thrown in jail." He said no one could leave their car while waiting for a permit. The driver entered the car first after scaring the bee away, and we followed close behind. The soldier finally left us alone. About twenty minutes later, the Syrian authorities allowed us to drive into their country and resume our trip to Lebanon.

Nearly five hours of waiting at the Syrian border left us sweaty, hungry, and thirsty. We were also over-come with fatigue from our early morning journey but had to persevere. We continued driving toward Lebanon through Damascus, the Syrian capital. Large numbers of police officers roamed the middle of that city, staring down drivers and pedestrians. Many military vehicles filled with Syrian soldiers parked on the side of the roads.

A few hours later, we quickly crossed through the Lebanese checkpoint. Once inside my native Lebanon, the geographic picture changed with a varied green, lush hills, colorful flowers, and mountains whizzing by through the car window. The air smelled fresher in Leb-anon. There were no patches of brown desert sand or violent dust storms like in Jordan and no pungent smells and garbage piles along the roads like in Syria.

It was early afternoon when we approached Beirut. Mom suggested to Mr. Musa that we stop somewhere for lunch. We came upon a town called Khaldeieh, just outside Beirut and on our way to the southern part of the country. Sitting at an outdoor cafe, we took in the astounding view of the Mediterranean beaches. The beach lay less than thirty feet away from us. I noticed bikini-clad young women just twenty feet away from our table. First, I thought I was hallucinating. I rubbed my eyes to make sure they weren't fooling me. I saw more gorgeous young Lebanese women sunbathing near the water's edge when I took my hands away. This cannot be real, I told myself. I kept thinking I had found paradise. In Mafraq, all women and girls covered up their bodies, and here all the women and girls were showing off their bodies. I couldn't remember if I had seen girls in Lebanon on the beach or not. If I had, that sight had not affected me as it did now.

The temperature dropped as we climbed the Lebanese mountain roads and continued to reach higher elevations in the south. The cool, refreshing air woke us up and gave us the energy to enjoy the sights.

It was about 4:00 PM when we approached Ein Eble, where my parents were from. Mountains surrounded the village. Apple, fig, peach, apricot, plum, and olive trees grew alongside the grapevines that covered most mountainsides. Like ours, many of the houses near our summer home had red-tiled roofs, with barns for cattle.

I got up from bed sleepy-eyed the following day and went to the balcony to join my family, drinking hot Selaney Indian tea we had brought with us from Jordan. Unlike Mafraq mornings, the air in Ein Eble had quite a chill to it. My family watched the camels with their colorful saddles, men perched atop Arabian horses, cows carrying huge, clear plastic bags full of tobacco leaves and hay on their backs, and meandering sheep, their shiny wool brushed to the side, filter past our balcony.

I saw farmers with goats and camels walking down the village's main road to the market.

My summers in Ein Eble were usually quiet, as I had no friends there. Although I had several relatives who lived in the village,I socialized with my grandma Sittie, my grandfather Jeddie, and cousin Laila. I developed a massive crush on her, but she hardly noticed me as she had friends close to her age. Laila's summer home in Ein Eble was less than a half-block away. Though our houses were close, an emotional gulf separated her family and mine. Even though our families rarely communicated, Laila and I continued to be friends despite our parents' disapproval. We snagged moments when we could. We used to sit on the ground watching Sittie make saj bread on a large metal dome outside her kitchen or have picnics in the nearby orchards.

I cherished the time I spent with Jeddie. He was a strong, outgoing older man with an infectious spirit. Jeddie took me riding with him on his horses, donkeys, and camels. I sat behind him on his horse many days, hugging his waist with my little hands, dropping my forehead onto his back, and listening to him whistle. I was delighted at the sight and smell of the wildflowers sprouting everywhere. Once we reached the windy trail of a nearby mountain, Jeddie sang old Lebanese love songs, some of which were sad, and told stories about saying goodbye to a loved one, which reminded me of Sana. Grandpa loved birds. He told me that the robins, wrens, and doves reminded him of angels and symbols of freedom. We often stopped under a fruit tree to have a picnic.

By the time the summer was over, I was ready to go back to Mafraq to be with my monkey, Sana, and Baba. I was nervous about facing the ALF, though, as I wasn't sure what they planned to do to my family or me after my abrupt departure.

We left Ein Eble to return to Jordan on the third Friday of August. Telephones did not exist in Mafraq or Ein Eble, so we had not heard a word from Baba the entire summer. The school would reopen on the first day of September. We took two buses from Ein Eble to Mafraq via Syria. My family and I managed to sit together in the back of both buses.

The bus engine roared underneath us, making the back of the bus especially noisy. My whole family was able to fall asleep except for me. However, it wasn't long before I fell asleep, and the last thing I remembered was arriving in Beirut. We took another bus in Beirut to go to Jordan. The bus had a Syrian license plate as well as a Syrian driver. Although there were about twenty passengers on the bus, it took less than an hour to have our papers authorized to enter Syria and continue to Jordan. Entering Syria from the Lebanese border was much smoother than entering from the Jordanian border. The relationship between Syria and Lebanon was favorable, and our driver was Syrian, not Jordanian.

Mama had brought sandwiches of *zahtar* with her.

We all ate on the bus while waiting for the Syrian soldiers' permission to enter their country. Soon after we finished our sandwiches, the bus driver returned with our legal documents. Hoisting himself into his seat, he continued driving toward Jordan.

Shortly after the bus started rolling, we all drifted back to sleep. When I opened my eyes, the bus had stopped, once again, at the border between Syria and Jordan. I was shocked to see many Syrian tanks massed at the border with their guns aimed toward Jordan. Mama immediately told us to keep our mouths shut. The Syrian army gave each passenger a difficult time as they attempted to uncover the purpose of each individual's trip. One of the soldiers coldly opened our suitcase and emptied everything onto the ground. One of my sisters asked why he was doing this. He responded he was just doing his job. When she asked him what kind of job, he shouted at her, "If you don't shut your mouth, I will cut out your tongue!"

Mama instantly shouted at my sister to remain silent. I glared at the soldier's face. I felt like attacking him, grabbing his gun, and shooting him in the ass. The soldiers spent more than two hours searching the bus and its passengers. The waiting period on the border was much less than what we experienced when we entered Syria coming from Jordan.

After what seemed like an eternity, we crossed into Jordan. It was the first time I ever felt as if Jordan was my true home. This was the country where I was born and raised; and where Sana, Baba, and my house were located. In the distance, we could see Jordanian tanks sitting at the border with their guns menacingly facing Syria. The Syrian tanks outnumbered the Jordanian tanks. Jordan and Syria were about to go to war.

Mafraq looked deserted. There were no signs of life, but we did see pictures of Syrian President Nureddin al-Atassi, Iraqi President Ahmad Hassan Al-Baker, and PLO leader Yasser Arafat hanging on almost every structure in Mafraq. I asked my mother why pictures of leaders from other countries were taped on Jordanian's city walls. She did not answer but looked at me with worried eyes. After the bus driver dropped us at the station, we walked home. Mama walked in the middle between my sisters, who walked behind my brothers and me. This was the tradition; women walked behind men. We walked for about ten minutes without seeing a soul on Mafraq's streets. It was late afternoon, but it might as well have been the middle of the night.

Baba was not there when we arrived home. It seemed he had not been at home for the last several days. The house looked filthy, and there was dust everywhere. A strange odor wafted from the backyard of our house. We were wary and curious about its origins. One of my sisters shouted at Mama, "Why did we come back to this hellish town? I told you we should not have come back to Jordan!" Her chest was heaving, and her round face flushed a warrior red.

"I am terrified," she continued. "I do not know

where Baba is, and I don't know where that damn smell is coming from."

I was the first to step out into the yard, my heart racing. I saw our little monkey, Sana, dead on the ground. Her body was riddled with bullet holes. I began to howl so loudly that I thought I would lose my voice. I tripped and fell onto the ground, screaming for my poor Sana.

I shouted, "I am going to kill the killer! I am going to kill the killer!" I sat next to Sana and cradled her stiff head between my little hands. Her innocent eyes were shut. Her lips were parted slightly, so I could see some of her teeth as if she were smiling at me. Her black, elegant-looking nose was dried out. I lowered my head to hers and kissed her forehead several times. Then I gently laid her body on the ground, my right palm under her head for a pillow. I held her hands between my own and asked her, "Why? Why, Sana? Who did this?" I began to rock back and forth. I cursed God and prayed, "Oh God, please have mercy on us. Oh, God, why? She was a little angel! Why did you allow this to happen? I used to believe in you! Why didn't you stop them? I thought you had the power to stop them!"

I asked her to forgive me for not taking her with us to Ein Eble. I told her I had saved some of my sandwiches for her.

"Oh, Sana, please wake up," I pleaded. "I need you more than you could ever imagine."

Mama approached me, knelt on her knees, and held my left arm between her hands. She was crying. She rose slightly off the ground, gently pulled me to her, and held me tighter than I could ever remember.

Sana had been dead for a few days. We had not been back in Mafraq for more than an hour and were already facing death. I held Mama tight and begged her to take us back to Ein Eble. I cried, "I can't take it anymore. I can't live like this anymore. Please help us; please take us back to Ein Eble. I am going to lose my mind in this town. I have already lost my friends, Maneh and Amjad. I lost my soul when Adel was killed, lost my hope when Abu Salah was assassinated, and now I will surely lose my mind after Sana."

My oldest brother spoke up. "It is all your fault. I am sure the ALF members shot Sana to hurt you. They knew you were attached to her. You are the reason for Sana's death. God is going to punish you for it."

My brother was right; since I used to bring sweet Sana to ALF headquarters, they knew how close I was to her. I was sure the ALF had retaliated against me by killing my Sana.

I shouted, "Oh God, I am sorry. Oh Sana, I am so sorry!" Sana's blood was still in my mouth from kissing her body. "It is all my fault that you were killed. It should have been me and not you, my baby. I am going to kill the killer. I am going to take revenge for my baby. Her blood is not going to be shed so easily and cheaply."

Mama tried to calm me down, saying, "No, Sana's death wasn't your fault, it was the militia's fault, and I hope God will take revenge on them."

"God? What God?" I shouted, "Do you think he would allow a massacre if God existed? Where was God when the killer shot Sana? Was he sleeping, or was he on a break? What God are you talking about?"

Mama looked hard at me with her tear-laden eyes. "Son, please don't talk about God like this. Remember, things could have been a lot worse than --"

I interrupted her, "Nothing is worse than this. Nothing."

My family was overcome with grief, crying hysterically. Mama ordered both of my sisters to knock at our neighbors' doors and ask if they had seen my Baba lately. This effort was futile; none of the neighbors answered their door. I felt as if we were the only people in town.

Mama suggested we go to Baba's clinic to find him. We began walking toward the clinic. Together we formed a united front. Pictures of the Syrian and Iraqi presidents were plastered to nearly every surface. We had no idea what had happened. The only thought that occupied our minds was finding Baba.

I became very nervous when we neared the ALF headquarters. Mama warned me before we approached the building to keep my eyes on the ground to avoid looking in the direction of the place that was once like a home to me. My sisters, who had very independent minds, stared defiantly at the building. They noticed it was devoid of human life. All of the Palestinian flags were gone from the building's roof. It was odd to see the building looking abandoned without noise filling its walls.

111

Our pace quickened as we saw four men in their thirties start towards us from the opposite direction. They carried guns. Ammunition and grenades dangled from belts around their waists. They ordered us to stop. One of them pointed his Russian gun several inches from Mama's forehead. Mama's face blanched. I started to tremble inside and was utterly terrified. The men asked us where we were going. We explained we were looking for Baba. I noticed the four men wore a patch with an emblem sewn onto the right arm of their shirts. The emblem depicted a soldier with "Palestinian Asefah Revolution" written under the picture. Asefah was a Palestinian militia group affiliated with the PLO. The man pointing the gun at Mama's head ordered us to return home. He said there was a curfew in Mafraq, active for the last few days. Mama explained we had just returned from Lebanon after being away for almost three months and did not know what was happening. She told them none of our neighbors were home, and we were only trying to find Baba. One of them screamed at her, ordering us to return home because the streets were not safe. Another man said they were planning to liberate Mafraq from the imperialists. He yelled they were planning to get rid of the traitor Hussein and his soldiers.

Disappointed, we quickly walked back home. We were shocked and felt ignorant about what was happening around us. We moved to the relative safety of the bathroom. It was secure because it had two different ceilings, making it safer during a potential airstrike. Also, since the bathroom was at the end corner of the house, it would take the militia longer to find us. The smell of poor Sana, whose remains were still outside, was overpowering. We sat on the floor of this small space as we had done a few short months ago, using the narrow walls as a place of refuge. My sisters huddled on the floor close to Mama while my brothers and I squeezed next to the opposite wall. Mama ordered us to stay quiet. She did not want the militia to hear us talking. The air was very still, except for the occasional whimper of one of my sisters.

We stayed in the same position on that bathroom floor for a couple of days. We had to leave, though, when one of us needed to use the facilities inside that tiny room. Our meals consisted of bread we brought from Ein Eble and dried parsley we kept in a jar in the kitchen. Sleeping was nearly impossible in the cramped confines of our little prison.

Early one morning, after being in Mafraq for three nights, we heard a car pulling up next to the house. We heard at least two men talking outside the front door. Alarmed at what might happen, we held our breaths and waited. The men softly knocked at our door. Mama told us not to move. She ordered us to stay silent. One of the men called in a low voice that they had come to help us contact Baba. Both men identified themselves, and Mama recognized them at once as two Jordanian Bedouin men we all knew. They were my Baba's friends and patients. Mama walked towards the door, and we tentatively followed. She cautiously opened the door to allow the men to enter. They were in their fifties and wore typical Bedouin garb with guns clutched in their hands.

They told us Baba was in Kufranja, Jordan, where my sister, Aida, lived with her husband and their children. The men said they had been monitoring our whereabouts since Baba left Mafraq seven days earlier. As soon as the conditions were relatively safe, they had every intention of helping us reconnect with Baba. He asked them to help us get to Kufranja when we returned from Lebanon.

This news thrilled us to the depths of our hearts; it was as if the sun had finally shown itself from behind the black clouds on our foreheads. The men were kind enough to help us bury Sana next to the olive tree in our backyard. Using our ax, we dug a little grave for Sana. Part of me was buried under the ground forever with Sana's lifeless body. While the men poured dirt into the grave, I cried uncontrollably. I spoke silently to Sana. "Thank you for all the joy and happiness you brought to my life. Thank you for the love you gave me. Thank you for the strength you brought me. Thank you for being there for me whenever I needed to talk to you."

The Jordanian men left after they buried Sana. We agreed to ready ourselves that night to go with the two men and join Baba at Aida's house. The men returned that night. We loaded ourselves into their jeep and drove away from our house with the headlights turned off. The inky darkness swarmed around us as we went through the streets of Mafraq, scared to the core of our souls.

On the way out of Mafraq, the Jordanian men told us they believed Syria was planning to invade Jordan. They also told us the Iraqi army already positioned in Jordan provided financial aid to some of the militia groups in Jordan to fight the Jordanian military. After Abu Ali mysteriously disappeared, the ALF collapsed and became part of the Palestinian Liberation Democratic People's Front. They said that Abu Ali had been gone since the beginning of July. I asked them if he had ever been found, and they answered in unison, "No." This news astonished me, and I felt sad for Abu Ali. I knew that Abu Ali didn't fit in the militia; he was too caring and gentle.

Mama interrupted my thoughts when she asked, "How can little Jordan stand by itself against Syria and the Palestinian militias?" The Bedouin men responded that the Israeli government would never agree to sit back with its hands folded, watching the Syrian army and the Palestinian militia killing the Jordanians. The men added that the Jordanians would love to see Mrs. Golda Meir's government and army destroy all the foreign armies in Jordan. The idea scared me but planted a small hope inside in my heart.

The driver turned the jeep's headlights back on as we exited the city, and we continued bucking and bolting along Jordan's semi-paved country roads. In northern

Jordan, we arrived at the next town, Irbid, relieved to see the Jordanian army in the streets and Jordanian flags waving from flag posts. Despite the darkness, we could see King Hussein's pictures on the walls of buildings. A couple of times, Jordanian army units stopped us. They were very polite and helpful, especially when they found Jordanian Bedouins in the Jeep. The Jordanian soldiers looked weary. Some yawned or napped inside their trucks, while others lazily drank coffee and smoked. They were a less powerful military force than the Syrian army and the Palestinian militias. After Lebanon, the Jordanian army was the smallest of the Arab countries bordering Israel.

We were ecstatic to arrive at Aida's and join her family and Baba. Aida's home was a stand-alone concrete structure with two bedrooms and an outdoor kitchen and bathroom located at the edges of Kufranja. Baba told us later that evening that Sana had disappeared from the house a couple of days before he fled Mafraq. He didn't know who had kidnapped her from the backyard of our home, but he had spent two whole days looking for her without success before coming to Kufranja.

After a late-night dinner at my sister's house, the Bedouin men returned to Mafraq. Kufranja had come under Jordanian army control. Unlike Mafraq, Kufranja appeared and felt a lot safer. During our first few days in town, we heard radio reports that there had been skirmishes between the Jordanian army and the Palestinian militia groups throughout Jordan. We also learned that the Palestinian militia had gained control of several strategic positions in Jordan, including the oil refinery near Az Zarqa, a Jordanian town close to Amman.

7
BLACK SEPTEMBER

ON SEPTEMBER 6, 1970, the Popular Front for the Liberation of Palestine (PFLP), led by George Habash, hijacked three planes; a TWA, Swissair, and Pan Am jet. Each plane was forced to land in the Jordanian desert. More than one hundred Western passengers were traveling aboard the three aircraft. Hearing this news made me sick to my stomach. Although I didn't realize it, this event was one of the most significant acts of terrorism globally. I remembered how my family was harassed at the Syrian border by its soldiers. The Western hostages were undergoing more severe harassment by the Palestinian gangs. It was small comfort to me that my family and I understood the language of the Syrian soldiers, but the hijacked passengers were indeed unable to comprehend the Palestinian gangs.

I asked Baba how these gangs could get away with this kind of inhumane behavior. He said, "They are not going to get away with it. We need a strong army here to help us get rid of these bastards. We need America's military power. We need Israel. We need Mrs. Gold Meir." A staunch disbeliever in Western customs, my father's words were astonishing. I agreed with Baba, although I wasn't sure if he meant what he said. I later understood that Baba's change of heart was due in part to his ties to the medical care field. He felt the plane passengers were innocent and should not have been subjected to a terrorist act. My dad became such a strong supporter of King Hussein that he declared he would back any country that promoted King Hussein, including America.

By mid-September, King Hussein of Jordan reinstated martial law and attacked all the PLO militia throughout Jordan. My parents were wary. They stayed huddled around the radio to hear the news updates every ten minutes. A rumor ran like wind around Kufranja that Israel was planning to take over Jordan while the Jordanian army and Palestinian militia were killing each other. Because Kufranja was close to the Israeli border, Baba suggested we pack and return to Mafraq. Our trip to Mafraq would take place during the Jordanian civil war, but Baba insisted Mafraq was safer than Kufranja. My sister's family had a bit of money to spare and helped support us in buying food and the essentials.

In mid-September 1970, we returned to Mafraq to avoid the rumored Israeli invasion. My entire family, including my sister Aida, her husband Peter, their three children, and our driver, squeezed into a little Toyota and set out for Mafraq.

Despite our intention to avoid the Israeli invasion, we instead found ourselves facing Syria's onslaught along the northern border of Jordan. Irbid looked like a city conjured out of a nightmare dreamt by the devil himself. Whistling shells, screaming bombs, fiery grenades, and exploding rockets rained down. Large columns of foul-smelling smoke rose and bled through the sky in downtown Irbid. The smell of charred remains and the blinding light from the fires in Irbid permeated every orifice. Aida's children cried loudly while we tried to keep them calm. An Arabic country trying to occupy another was a bizarre phenomenon.

Omar, the driver, moved forward despite the shelling and bombs that fell around us. My body quaked uncontrollably. Although I was scared, I thought I was lucky because I would die with the people I loved the most instead of dying alone like many other people. As we moved farther away from Irbid, the intensity of the shelling and bombing lessened. The thirty miles between Irbid and Mafraq felt like a thousand.

As we approached Mafraq, we noticed Iraqi army personnel and machinery moving away from Mafraq, heading towards their own country. Their monstrous equipment plowed through the desert, leaving behind a billowing trail of dust. We were shocked to see the Iraqis leaving Jordan so quickly. I remember Baba saying, "If the Iraqis continue to depart Jordan peacefully, I believe the Jordanian army will stand against the Syrian army alone. I was only concerned about the Jordanian army going to war with Syria and Iraq. I think the Jordanian army is going to wipe out the Syrians." A silence settled in the car after Baba finished talking.

Once we arrived in Mafraq, we found it strangely quiet again, like when we returned from Lebanon. The Iraqi army barely had a presence in Mafraq since they moved their machinery and personnel back to Iraq. Two days after we arrived in Mafraq, the Iraqi military had almost completely vanished. The heavy fighting between the Jordanian and Syrian armies continued in the northern part of the country, and fighting between the Jordanian army and Palestinian militia groups endured all over Jordan. Mafraq was spared this time and remained quiet even though the Palestinian militia noticeably controlled it.

Three days after the Iraqi army disappeared from Mafraq, the Jordanian Bedouins declared war against the Palestinian militia in Mafraq. The Jordanian army was busy fighting the Palestinian guerrillas in other cities and towns in Jordan. Although the Palestinian militias were better equipped than the Bedouins, many Palestinian troops moved out of Mafraq to support other militias in cities and towns across Jordan. The battles between the Bedouins and the Palestinian militias lasted barely three days before the Jordanian Bedouins kicked all the Palestinian gangs out of Mafraq. It was mainly pistol fighting. There weren't any bombs used in this battle. We didn't have to stay in the bathroom. Sometimes we stood in the street listening to the shooting since the fighting was only a couple of blocks away.

Right after the Palestinian militia left Mafraq, some of our neighbors, and my family, danced in the streets. We celebrated the Bedouin victory but noticed several warplanes flying low above Mafraq toward the border of Syria. None of us knew who these jets belonged to, but rumors indicated Pakistan. Other gossip asserted they were Israeli warplanes flying in to help the Jordanians liberate their land from the Syrians. Still, more people claimed they were American and British jets aiding the Jordanian army against Palestinians and Syrians. Letting several radios blare the news, we continued celebrating in the streets. The news reports chattered updates of the events unfolding around Jordan but failed to report on the planes that nipped northward. Jordanian women and children rallied in the Mafraq streets, chanting, "Thank you, thank you, Golda Meir! Help, help, Israel!"

The Jordanians in Mafraq concluded the war jets must be Israeli. Still scared and hearing the explosions from bombing in neighboring towns, we cheered the Israeli government, helping us end the Syrian invasion. My Baba and other Jordanian men who joined the celebration in the streets repeated, "Today is historic. Our long-time enemy, Israel, came and saved our lives when our Arab nations attacked us." Neither the Jordanian government nor the media ever admitted that Israeli warplanes were helping Jordan, but the Jordanians in Mafraq were utterly convinced that Israel was now their ally. My emotions were conflicted. The Israeli planes, which killed two of my friends, were now the reason for my family and me and other Jordanians to survive the onslaught. It was hard for me then to understand these events. Baba used to tell me the enemy of my enemy was my friend. His words did not explain how we had become so friendly with our long-time enemy.

The skilled warplane fighters defended the Jordanians against the Syrians for days and nights of the following week. The majestic planes annihilated the Syrian military and forced Syria to pull back to their own country. In the meantime, the Jordanian military continued fighting the Palestinian militia in Jarash, Ajloon, Zarqa, and Amman, destroying most of them.

Several thousand people died in Jordan during the month-long civil war. In those September days of unrest, food became scarce. We ate lentils and lima beans for breakfast and lunch for more than ten consecutive days. Our dinners consisted of bread, parsley, and grape leaves. Because the militia controlled the stores in Mafraq, they took all the food with them when they left. Food was more valuable than gold in Mafraq. Sometimes, the hunger pains in my stomach kept me awake all night. By the end of September, the Jordanian forces entered Mafraq, and food became available to everyone. Though the civil war raged for only thirty days, it felt like a war I had fought my whole life.

Jordanian schools reopened in October. I was in the seventh grade with new teachers and classmates. In every class, we discussed the civil war endlessly. We hardly learned anything the whole year since, in every class, the only subject was our hero King Hussein who was able to crush all the Palestinian parties and the Syrian army. Every teacher and student was on the King's side and referred to him as our hero. Everybody at school was happy that year since we had all survived the deadly civil war. Students smiled the entire year since they hardly had any homework. The only homework was telling stories about the war and the strong Jordanian army that won the conflict.

One evening at the dinner table, Baba said he heard that a teacher he knew from Amman had lost his only two brothers during the war. One of the brothers had been a soldier with the Jordanian army and had died in Zarqa fighting the militia. His other brother was a member of the Palestinian Liberation Organization killed in Amman fighting against the Jordanian army.

One week before school let out in May, the teacher committed suicide. He shot himself in the head at his home and left a note that read, "No one won, we all lost."

We heard the sad news about my grandmother, Sittie, who passed away in Lebanon in mid-February. I was devastated. The end of the school year came as a relief. I hoped we would go to Ein Eble again for the summer. But Baba informed us he would not send us to Lebanon that year because he was short on money.

I knew I would desperately miss Laila and Jeddie that summer.

Baba had left us again to work in Saudi Arabia by the end of June. We all hated the idea and didn't want him to leave us once more. He promised he would be back for Christmas. His promise calmed me down, hopeful of better things to come. Mama assured me the time between June and December would fly. I spent the summer of that year playing soccer with some friends or playing war, one team against another. We used stones as our weapons, pelting each other. The game was dangerous, and Mama never approved of me playing. I played the game anyway. My arm was strong, and I was an accurate stone thrower. I became popular among the Mafraq kids; some feared my arm. I often hit the target perfectly, and usually, the target was another kid.

During the last week of July, I was playing as usual when I hit another kid in his leg. He fell to the ground, hurt. His older brother came after me and shot me with a BB gun. The pellet hit me in the right eye, but luckily the gun was loaded with wheat seed instead of actual BB pellets. Blood poured from the gash, leaving me unable to see. The pain was searing and darted through me like a stream of electricity. I ran home as fast as I could and shouted for my mother. She nearly fainted when she saw my eye bleeding. After washing the wound, she, with the help of some neighbors, rushed me to a hospital in Amman.

The hospital was small. There were four or five large rooms for patients with about twenty beds inside. There was only one nurse for each room. The room where I stayed smelled bad. Two British physicians worked on my eye, and I was hospitalized for a week. Luckily, my sight was restored, but my days as a stone warrior ended. I found out later the boy I hit was okay. And his brother and parents came to our home to apologize to Mama and me. The rest of my summer was spent watching my Mama and sisters clean and cook at home.

In September, I welcomed returning to school; it felt exciting to be in the eighth grade. My favorite subject in school was girls, in addition to mathematics. Math kept my brain working while girls kept my heart beating. During those months between September and December, while I waited impatiently for Baba to arrive home, I spent much of my free time thinking about girls and discovering myself. I was restless and excited by all the new feelings my body was experiencing.

Christmas arrived without my Baba. He sent us a Christmas note in a telegraph that read he would be with us in the coming summer. He stated his employer wouldn't allow him a vacation yet, as he had only been there a short time. Baba's note broke my heart and killed my hope. I wasn't happy with Baba for not showing up, but I learned to live with it. I kept myself busy with school and the new fascination with my body, waiting anxiously for summer. When summer arrived, Mama decided we should stay in Mafraq to wait for Baba. The days ticked by, measured by the weight of our vigil. Baba had let us down again. Baba's decision didn't hurt me;

it hardly affected me. Instead, my heart, broken since Christmas time, turned to stone.

The following September greeted me a year older without seeing my father or visiting Ein Eble. I started the new school year feeling depressed, like a failure without my Baba. I took pleasure and escaped from my heartache by looking at girls and relieving the bulge in my crotch. Young women were small doses of happiness. They made me forget how sad and disappointed I was, and I began to feel special about being in the ninth grade. It was my last grade in the Christian school.

A telegram arrived from Baba in the last week of May. He asked us to meet him in Ein Eble during the summer. We were excited. Mama packed for everybody, singing and humming while filling up the suitcases with clothes. She was as happy as a little girl with a new doll. We left for Ein Eble the second week of June. Ein Eble didn't feel right with Sittie gone and without Laila, who was no longer spending her summers in Ein Eble. The town and its beauty were not the same.

That summer in Ein Eble was long and dreary. Jeddie was sick. He had pain in both his legs and his diabetes was out of control. Everything that had been familiar about Ein Eble had changed completely. Adding to my despondence was my father's absence; he never showed up. Mama was angry and discouraged. We returned to Mafraq the last week of August.

That September, I started tenth grade in the only

high school in Mafraq for boys. It was a government school called Mafraq Secondary Boys School. This school was a lot different than the Christian school. It was housed in an old building. The students were grungy and smelled bad. Some of them looked as if they had never taken a bath. The smell of rotten eggs permeated the decrepit building. At first, I hated everything about it. It took me several months to adjust, and I made a few Muslim friends there. Many times they indicated they wished I was a Muslim like them. Whenever they spoke about me not being Muslim, I said, "At least I am lucky I have friends like you who are Muslim."

On Christmas day of that year, my Baba returned from Saudi Arabia. His long absence was due to his employer refusing to give him vacation time. This was not unusual in Saudi Arabia. When Baba returned, he decided to open up a clinic in Mafraq just like a few years ago, and we were all happy he was back. My oldest brother, Basem, left for Italy to attend college two months later. It was not unusual for Middle Eastern young people to go to western countries to receive their education.

I was not bothered that Basem left. I knew I would not miss him and had never felt close to him. We were so different, and I thought I had never gotten to know him. He had a very volatile temper and often hurled objects at my mom, siblings, and me. While my dad was in Saudi Arabia, Basem and Mama fought because she refused to let him smoke in the house. He threw a pair of scissors at her, striking her left foot. One of my sisters and I helped Mama pull the scissors out. She had to take medication and stay off her feet for several weeks.

At the end of the school year, I decided to be a mathematician or an engineer. I had liked math ever since I was a young child. It was the only subject I didn't need to study and seemed to understand naturally. Solving math problems for me was as much fun as playing soccer. I thought I wanted to teach math to little students. I imagined myself as a teacher in a classroom with kids surrounding me, learning this mysterious but fun subject.

That summer, I worked for my Baba. I did housekeeping work in his clinic, sweeping and mopping the floor whenever needed. I became closer to Baba, but I liked meeting and talking to his female patients, especially those my age.

I met Alia at the clinic in mid-July. She looked as if a master artist had drawn her. Her hazel eyes were magical portals, her smile was peerless, and her dark brown hair fell in waves of fine silk. I felt little jolts of energy whenever my eyes and hers met. I found out we were in the same grade. She went to Mafraq Secondary Girls' School, a government high school for girls in Mafraq. She coughed while we talked and told me she had the flu. I wished I were a doctor to cure her and felt jealous Baba was her doctor. She told me she loved poetry and hated math. She said her father had a store in Mafraq and asked if I had ever been there. She also told me her parents were not planning to send her to college because they believed college was only for boys. Her voice moved through me like angels' music. I told her I loved math, and it was my favorite subject, but I don't think she was impressed.

My Baba wrote her a prescription. She started to leave the clinic, with one foot outside, one inside, when she turned to me and said, "I could use some help in math sometime."

I answered her without thinking, "Yes, me, too; I can use some help whenever you want to."

She laughed and continued on her way. I felt foolish about my answer but excited about seeing her again. It wasn't until September, when school reopened, that I saw Alia. We noticed each other in the streets, and exchanged looks.

I decided to break the ice one day and said, "Hello."

I was surprised when she said, "Hi," adding, "What took you so long?" Her melodious voice echoed in my ears for the rest of the day. Each time we passed each other, we secretly exchanged greetings. I used to see her twice a day, once in the morning on my way to school and once in the afternoon on my way home. The Mafraq high school for boys was located northwest of the town, while the girls' high school was located in the southeast section. Alia always wore the same uniform. It was a dress with white and blue stripes, reaching her knees. Under the dress, she wore black pants, a uniform similar to other high school girls in Jordan. But on Alia, the simple uniform looked like elegant evening wear. A few weeks passed when we began to write small notes.

A boy and girl could only communicate by writing a note and discretely handing it over. The young man would be thrown in jail if the couple was caught. Dating and sexual activity did not exist before marriage. A bride must be a virgin at her wedding. If a bride was found to have been defiled, she could face death by her father or relatives. Usually, if a man killed his daughter or his sister for not being chaste, he would not be punished nor sent to trial for murder. It was understood he had washed out the shame of his family. Kissing a girl in Muslim society could result in five years in prison.

The notes we passed were carefully folded inside a tiny piece of paper. She never missed catching them. Once on my way home after school, Alia threw a note to me, and I missed it. Two older men witnessed me bending down to pick the note up. They approached me to take it away and wanted to report me to the police. Acting quickly, I put the note in my mouth, chewed, and swallowed to hide the evidence. The men searched me completely in the street, looking for the note. Though they could not find it, they reported me to the police anyway. The following morning, the police came to my class, searching my desk and pockets for the note. When they couldn't find it, they took me to their station, stripped me, and searched for the note. I was embarrassed to be naked. Unable to find a shred of evidence, the police released me several hours later.

I went back to school. I didn't feel ashamed of what the police had done because it happened to nearly every student in the school. Some students felt proud and macho whenever the police picked them up for writing a note to a girl.

Despite the police incident, Alia and I continued to exchange notes. Usually, after reading a note from Alia, I hid it inside my underwear until I found a safe and deserted place to burn it. This way, I was sure neither one of us would ever get in trouble. Alia would do the same thing.

One morning I decided to give Alia a red rose Mama had planted in our backyard. I hid the rose under my left sleeve. I threw the rose to her when Alia came close by, but she didn't expect it and missed the flower. The rose fell to the ground, and Alia kneeled to grab it. We were both caught by other students. I knew for sure I would be in trouble with the Jordanian authorities. Three hours later, the Jordanian police came to my school and took me to their headquarters for interrogation. I denied giving Alia the rose, lying so I would not go to jail.

The police officers insisted that witnesses saw me giving Alia the rose. I continued denying it and reiterated they were mistaken. After two hours of questioning, the police brought Alia and her father in. When Alia saw me, her face became as red as the rose I threw her that morning. She was scared. When the police asked her about the rose, she told them she had no idea what they were talking about. Alia had gotten me out of big trouble. The officer slapped me a couple of times and sent me back to school. The ordeal was a great lesson for both of us. I vowed I would never throw a rose at her again. She decided never to see or deal with me again. She changed the route she took to avoid seeing me. I never saw her again.

In January of 1975, my Baba informed us he was planning to go back to Saudi Arabia to work for the third time, as the pay was much better than in Jordan. Baba said he was not making the money he made before in Mafraq. Mama said if Baba went to Saudi Arabia, she would move to Lebanon with the children. He didn't care much for her decision, but she didn't care for his decision either. They decided that Mama, my older brother Muneer, and my two older sisters would go to Lebanon first. I would join them as soon as I finished high school in Mafraq. Splitting up the family made me feel strange, and I didn't like it. I didn't want to be alone in the house in Mafraq. Mama convinced me, saying it was the only way to move back to her country. She had been waiting for this chance for more than twenty-five years. I understood but dreaded living alone for the entire year.

In the first week of September 1975, Baba returned to Saudi Arabia, and the rest of my family moved to Beirut. I stayed in Mafraq to finish the school year.

Mama said as soon as she found an apartment in Beirut, she would send me a telegraph with the address so I could join them in June when I graduated.

After everyone had gone, the loneliness set in. I missed the noises of Mama cleaning the dishes in the kitchen. I missed the rattle of the sewing machine when my sisters sewed. I forgot my older brother's loud voice when he shouted at me for aggravating him. But most of all, I missed my Baba's thick, raised voice when he and Mama argued. I missed sharing the house with my family and the bedroom with my siblings. The nights were endless, interminable. Though I was home, I was homesick for my family. I consoled myself to think that I would see them in a year. I spent a lot of my last year in high school playing soccer with my classmates or thinking about girls—stealing looks at pictures of women in swimsuits in the pages of foreign magazines. When darkness came, the house's emptiness wrapped itself around me like a boa constrictor. I often had nightmares.

Mama had directed me to sell off the furniture in the house before I joined them in Lebanon. It made the house seem even more vacant, and the money I made from selling the pieces of furniture was hardly enough to buy food.

Cleaning up the kitchen became a significant challenge. I hated it. Cooking time was fun, though, even when I made mistakes. The first time I cooked a chicken, I forgot to clean out its insides and cooked it with its guts. The smell made me sick, and I had to throw my dinner away, going to bed hungry. At that time, Mafraq did not sell frozen chicken. The only chickens we ate were ones the butcher slaughtered. The cook was then responsible for removing its feathers and gutting the inside of the chicken. The second time I cooked chicken, I forgot about it while it was in the oven, and it burned. I sat next to Sana's grave in the backyard, watching the stars, when I smelled smoke coming from our house. The kitchen was a complete haze of smoke, and I had difficulty seeing the button to turn off the oven. The only meal I could cook expertly was an omelet with tomatoes and onion, as this is what I enjoyed watching Mama making at home. That was another night I went to bed hungry.

I heard from Mama in mid-April when she telegraphed me their new address. I felt relieved I would see my family again shortly. The last few weeks dragged by. I was anxious for them to end so I could move to Lebanon. A few days before school finished, I heard on the radio there was fighting between Palestinian militia groups and the Lebanese Christian militias inside Beirut. There was not enough information about the cause of the fighting or its purpose. I was concerned about traveling to Lebanon, but I had no choice because my family expected me. Besides, I was just about out of money, so there was no way I could spend the summer in Mafraq even if I wanted to.

8
REUNITED IN BEIRUT

I GRADUATED FROM HIGH SCHOOL IN MAY 1976 and celebrated my graduation alone in the backyard, sitting next to Sana's grave and wishing she was there. I sold the rest of the furniture for practically nothing to our neighbors. The only things that remained in the house were me and my suitcase. I learned how to be utterly independent by being alone at home during my senior year in high school. Even though I missed Mama, Baba, and my siblings, I found I was much stronger than I ever knew. On the third day of June, fourteen months after the civil war in Lebanon started, I traveled to Beirut. I was excited to see my family but worried about reports of fighting.

I took the bus from Mafraq to Irbid and then traveled by car service to Beirut. There were five of us, in addition to the driver. I alone was Lebanese. Before we left Irbid, the driver warned us about the fighting in Beirut. He said Lebanon was facing a deadly civil war similar to the one that raged a few years ago in Jordan, but perhaps more complicated, and it could last for a long time. None of the passengers responded. Two of the riders, a man and his wife, were Palestinians, and the other two, older men and brothers, were Jordanian. The Palestinian couple were traveling to visit relatives in Sidon, in southern Lebanon. The Jordanian brothers were going to the American University of Beirut Hospital because one was ill. The sick man and his brother sat next to the driver in the front. I sat scrunched up against the Palestinian couple next to me at the right rear door. It was a long, dusty ride. I closed my eyes to pass the monotonous drive.

Everyone in the car remained quiet. The car didn't even contain a radio. It took us a few hours to reach Damascus. The city was teeming with cars and pedestrians. It looked familiar to me, as I had been there before when I traveled to Lebanon with my family in the summer season. Pictures of Hafez Assad, the President of Syria, were glued and hung over Damascus' walls. Syrian soldiers were ubiquitous. The machinery and equipment of the militias looked as if the Syrian capital was putting on a military show just for us. Gradually, the car edged further away from Damascus in the direction of Lebanon.

My heart was seared with happiness when I finally saw the Lebanese sign at the border blazing, "AHLAN WASAHLAN," which meant welcome. Once we were in Lebanon, even the outside breeze changed – it became cleaner. The sky was perfectly blue, and the smell through the car windows was refreshing. I couldn't wait to see Mama and my siblings again. I wanted to smell her, kiss those hands that carried me when I was a baby, and hear the voice that sang me to sleep many nights.

We finally made it to Beirut and heard shooting. The civil war in Lebanon was between the Lebanese Christian militias against the Palestinian militias supported by the Lebanese Muslims. The gunfire was coming from inside Beirut, as well as the suburbs. I wasn't scared. I was able to tell the shooting wasn't nearby. I kept my thoughts focused on seeing my family.

The driver was kind enough to drop me at the stop to catch the bus from Beirut to Antonieh, where my Mama and siblings lived in a modest apartment a few miles southeast of Beirut. I waited in the street for less than ten minutes, hearing shooting and explosions in the distance, when the bus came. The bus was almost empty with only a few passengers. The bus driver explained there were some streets he might need to avoid because of the fighting. I asked the driver if the area was dangerous. He replied that all of Beirut and Lebanon were dangerous right now. I sat directly behind the driver and the other passengers sat in the back.

As the bus entered an area called Ein Al Rumaneh, explosions echoed all around us. I became apprehensive that my visit to Lebanon was a mistake. Some of the buildings were burning, their flames licking at the sky. Several men wearing military outfits and carrying machine guns ran down the street ahead of the bus. I kept quiet, my thoughts revolving around death. Not again, I pleaded to God. I had enough of that shit in Jordan. I didn't want to have anything to do with war anymore.

I turned to look at the passengers in the back, and they were all ducked under their seats. I wanted to do the same, but my curiosity wouldn't let me. The bus left the fighting area less than two minutes later. I felt relieved when the sound of shooting faded away. I thought, "I don't ever want to come back to Lebanon again if it is this dangerous here!"

I asked the driver, "What the hell is happening in our country?" He didn't answer, only saying he wasn't interested in talking politics.

We finally arrived in Antonieh. The bus driver dropped me within walking distance of my family's home. It was a nice and quiet neighborhood; there was no shooting in Antonieh. My family lived on the first floor of a four-story apartment building. The building looked good from the outside, painted dark tan with a maroon trim to look elegant. Beirut and Mafraq were so different; there was no comparison. Mafraq resembled an old, poor block next to Beirut.

I went inside the apartment building and took the stairs. Although there was an elevator, I didn't know how to use it, as I had never seen one before. Once I reached my family's apartment, I rang the doorbell. Mama was shocked when she opened the door and saw me. Her face lit up; she gave me a huge embrace and called my siblings. They had no idea if I would make it safely to

Lebanon because of all the fighting. I told them about the harrowing journey and how happy I was to see them after this tedious year. They were all glad I arrived safely.

My new family apartment had two bedrooms, a living room connected to the dining room, a kitchen, and one bathroom. The walls inside the apartment were clean and white. The floor was marbled, filled with different spots of bright color. The apartment was big enough for my entire family to live in comfortably. Mama had her bedroom; my two sisters slept in the other bedroom, my older brother slept in the dining room on a small bed next to the dining table, and I slept on the sofa in the living room. My Baba periodically sent money to my family in Beirut while working in Saudi Arabia.

Shortly after I arrived, we heard gunfire, and the explosions of bombs almost every day through the entire month of June, especially at night. Although it was evident that the shootings were not in Antonieh, they were close by and loud enough to keep us awake. It was too dangerous to travel around Lebanon that summer; we could not revisit Ein Eble.

My two sisters and older brother introduced me to some of the friends they had made in Antonieh over the past year. I was excited and looking forward to meeting their friends, only to find out I didn't fit well. Not only that, I even felt there was some unmeasured distance between my siblings and myself. I would have preferred to stay alone rather than hang out with my siblings and their friends. Shortly afterward, I found out I didn't fit well with Lebanese society. In Lebanon, almost everyone I knew smoked, drank Turkish coffee much of the day, and gossiped about their best friends and relatives – a lifestyle I could never get used to. I wished I was back in Mafraq on my own in that house. Mama was able to tell I was trying to isolate myself, but I kept denying it and assured her that everything was alright.

By the end of June, the shooting and shelling started to get closer and closer to us. The civil war between the Christian Phalangists and Muslim Palestinian militia had escalated to all of Beirut, including Antonieh. The sounds of explosions and machine guns petrified my family and me. Many days and nights, we thought our death was about to arrive.

Since our apartment was on the first floor of the building, all the residents who lived on the second, third, and fourth levels came down to our apartment. The Lebanese believed the lowest floor of a building was the safest place. Bullets, shells, and bombs hit some buildings in Antonieh, including the building my Aunt Waela lived in, about half a block away. That building was also a four-story structure. A bomb hit the fourth floor. Fortunately, no one was injured. Everyone had been hiding in the first-floor hallway of my aunt's apartment.

When the shelling stopped, our neighbors returned to their apartments. I emphasized to Mama we should all leave Lebanon. I told her it was enough that we had survived the war in Jordan. Mama said it was not easy to move again. She added that she was very happy in Lebanon. All her relatives lived there, and she planned to spend the rest of her life close to them. I told her I was not ready to die and wanted to leave and run away anywhere. I shouted, I was tired of war, shooting, and killing.

I began to think of a plan to escape from the deadly war. I decided to run away to Halab, Syria. I knew there was a college where I could study my favorite subjects, math, and physics. I hardly had any money, but I decided to go anyway. I thought about hitchhiking even though I knew it was dangerous. Staying in Lebanon and joining some organization to fight a war with no goal was even more dangerous.

I didn't want to join any war after my experience in Jordan. I also didn't wish Muneer to join any of the militias either. By militia standards, if we both were in the house, one would be forcefully drafted to join the Christian militias. But if I left Lebanon, Muneer most likely wouldn't have to participate in the civil war since he would be the only boy in the house. I determined the only way to evade the fight and have my brother avoid it was to run away from that hellish country, Lebanon.

I thought about Mama. I knew how much she loved Lebanon, but I didn't feel the same because I was born and grew up in Jordan. My heart broke thinking about running away, but neither the militia nor my family had given me much choice. I knew what was best for my brother and me and hoped they would understand. I decided that August would be the best time to leave Lebanon.

Beirut deteriorated between July and August, as Jordan had done six years before. The Palestinian militia and their allies, the Lebanese Muslim Shiite and Sunnis militia, had controlled more than seventy percent of Beirut. It was clear they were winning the war. The Lebanese Christian militia tried hard to stop the other militias. Each group accused the other of working against Lebanon. Sometimes the shelling lasted for five or six consecutive days, followed by a cease-fire for a day or two.

In Lebanon, the militia members would stop traffic on a major road and ask the drivers and passengers for identification. They checked the religion of each individual. It was easy to tell a person's religion in Lebanon: by either their name or picture identification card, which included their religion. Should the religion of the car occupants not be the same as the militiamen, they would be abducted, brought to an isolated area, and shot. This was only one of the ways people were killed during the civil war in Lebanon.

A cease-fire was declared in Lebanon in the middle of August 1976. I thought it was a perfect opportunity to escape to Syria, as it was the only Arab country that bordered Lebanon by land. On the last Sunday of August, my family and I went to church. I made sure to sit somewhere away from them in the back row. I attended the first half of the mass, ran home, and packed a shirt, a pair of pants, and underwear in a brown bag. I left a note to my family telling them I would always love them. I explained there was no future for me in Lebanon. I wrote that I was sick of wars and didn't want my brother or me to fight in a nonsense conflict. I felt awful but knew I was doing the right thing.

With one hundred Lebanese lira, about twenty American dollars at that time, in my pocket, I took a bus from Antonieh to downtown Beirut. It was just enough to get me to Syria. The bus ride to Beirut was about fifteen minutes. Once in Beirut, I rode in a car designated to carry passengers from Beirut to Damascus, Syria. I sat in the middle of the backseat. Next to me sat a Sunni Lebanese Muslim. The man was in his forties, and his name was Abdullah. On the other side of me sat an elderly, friendly Lebanese Shiite Muslim woman named Ayshah. I told her I was Lebanese Christian—supposedly an enemy to the Lebanese Muslims—, but she did not seem to mind. I called her "Khalty Ayshah," during the trip. *Khalty* means aunt in Arabic. It was impolite in Arabic culture to call an older adult by their first name.

Abdullah did not care for me. It was obviously due to my religion. I tried to make conversation with him, but he remained silent. Adnan, the driver, was also a Lebanese Sunni Muslim and didn't talk much during our trip. Ayshah and I made him smile easily, though, when we spoke to him. Sitting next to the driver was a

Lebanese Muslim Shiite named Ibraheem and his wife, Samira. They were both in their fifties and very friendly. I was quickly able to discern each person's religion from their names. Lebanese Christians and Muslims hardly shared the same first names.

I told them I was going to Syria to attend college in Halab. Samira said I must be a brave young man to go to Syria without knowing anyone there, especially being a Lebanese Christian. I thanked her for her compliment. Ibraheem asked my age. When I told him I was eighteen, he asked if I was sure I wanted to go to Syria and live there alone. I told him I would be safer in Syria than in Lebanon.

"At least there will not be any shooting, bombing, or shelling like there is in Beirut," I said. Everyone in the car agreed with me. Ayshah said she did not understand why anyone would shoot or try to kill their people. She thought all Lebanese were crazy with the way they acted. We all agreed with the older woman. I added that it was regrettable to sit and watch such a beautiful country burn.

Ibraheem said, "It is terrible that the Lebanese are destroying their own country." Abdullah scratched his head and said the Lebanese Christians were the ones who started this deadly war.

I did not respond. His words hurt me. Ayshah said it was the Palestinians' fault for this horrifying war. She said they were the ones who divided the Lebanese among themselves. I immediately agreed with the older lady and added they had done the same thing in Jordan.

I told them I was in Jordan during the war between the Jordanians, Palestinians, and Syrians. Ibraheem asked me what I was doing in Jordan, and I explained I was born in Jordan even though I was Lebanese. I told them I had just finished high school in Jordan and moved to Antonieh. Samira asked if I regretted moving to Lebanon in such a mess. I answered that we all left Jordan because Mafraq was a desert village, too small for my siblings and me to build a future. Beirut was a much larger and more prosperous city than Mafraq, but there was too much violence and unrest.

We finally entered Shtoora, the last town in Lebanon before the Syrian border. We noticed the main road to Syria was jammed with slow-moving cars. Adnan began to yield and finally had no choice but to stop completely. In the distance, several gunmen appeared, searching the vehicles in front of us.

Three militiamen came to our car. They had a Kalashnikov slung on their shoulders with a familiar-looking belt. Two of them stood in front of the vehicle while the other man stuck his head inside the driver's window. He asked us in a deep, loud voice with a Palestinian accent if there were any Christian people in the car. No one answered. I was panic-stricken. I started sweating as if I were sitting in a sauna. I made my eyes blank, keeping them aimed at the ground. The same man shouted again, "Is there any damn Christian person in this damn car?" We remained silent. He asked us for our passports. I could almost smell the foul scent of death, thinking this could be the last minute of my life.

He checked our passports and confirmed that I was a Christian. Beckoning to his partners, the three men turned around and gathered by Abdullah's side of the car, ordering me to get out. I waited for Abdullah to get out first. I started to get out of the car slowly, and when I had completely emerged, I could read a sign glued to the wooden part of one of the guns. It read "FATEH," which was part of the PLO. Abdullah and I stood outside the car. The Palestinian men ordered Abdullah to get back inside, but he refused. He told the militiamen he knew me and that I did not belong to any of the Christian militias, and they should not kidnap me. One militiaman said to Abdullah, "If you do not get inside the car, we will kill both of you." Abdullah got in the car instantly.

The man with the deep voice asked me why I did not identify myself when he asked if there were any Christians in the car. I did not answer. He asked me the same question again, but I still did not respond. I was too scared to talk. He picked up his gun from around his shoulder and jabbed me with the butt end in the stomach. I screamed and dropped to the ground on my knees. I heard one of the car doors open. I saw Khalty Ayshah trying to get out of the car. One of the Palestinian men shouted at her, ordering her to get inside or he would shoot her. She did not respond and continued walking toward me. The same militiaman screamed at her again, telling her that he would shoot me whether she entered the car or not. Khalty Ayshah went down on her knees next to me, put her arm around my shoulder, and said calmly, "That is fine, but you will have to shoot both of us."

One of the men yelled at her. "Are you crazy, old woman? Move away, or I will shoot."

"Go ahead; we are ready to be killed," Ayshah answered. I was both scared to death and impressed with Khalty Ayshah; I could not believe her bravery.

"What is wrong with you, old woman? Are you out of your mind or what?" another one of the gunmen shouted. "He is a Christian, and he should be killed. You are a Muslim like me. You should be on my side, not his."

My Lebanese heroine told them I was her neighbor in Beirut, and she had known me all my life and was a good friend of my grandmother. She added that she could never face my grandmother again if something happened to me. The militiamen asked her where she was going. She said she was going to Halab with me to introduce me to her son, who lived there. She told them I planned to live with her son while going to college in Halab.

My Lebanese friend saved my life and put on a great act. One of the men asked me if I were a member of the Phalangists. I told them I was born and raised in Jordan. I explained that I had been in Lebanon for only two months after finishing high school in Jordan. I almost blurted I had been a member of the ALF but decided against it because I feared they would call me a traitor, working against the Palestinians; a great excuse to kill me. The men ordered us to get in the car and continue our trip to Syria. Once inside the vehicle, Samira was crying, and her husband's face had turned the color of candle wax. The driver looked as if he had been crying or was just about to start. Abdullah was relieved to have us both in the car, again. I thanked Khalty Ayshah for saving my life and making up those great stories. She was smiling at me while tears rolled down her wrinkled face.

Saying goodbye to everyone in the car, especially Khalty Ayshah, was difficult once we arrived in Damascus. I held her hand between mine, kissed it, and brought it to my forehead with deep respect. With a quivering voice, I told her I would never forget her for saving my life.

I continued my trip to Halab on a small bus. When the bus finally arrived, night had fallen, and the college was closed. I did not have much money and wanted to save every penny, so I spent the night just outside the admissions office. I stretched out on the floor and made the brown bag with my clothes my pillow. The night air was warm, so I did not need any covers. Closing my eyes, I fell into an exhausted sleep.

It was early morning when I awoke to the sound of a barking dog. Several hours later, the admissions office opened. I met with the college officials and asked if I could enroll in the college math department. They gave me at least ten different forms to fill out before meeting with the head of the department. Once I filled out the forms, I was allowed to meet the chairman to determine if I was qualified to attend the college.

The chairman's name was Mr. Al-Mustafa. He was completely bald. He seemed to stare at me angrily. Although he was a short man, his ample stomach made him hard to ignore. He threw himself on his chair behind his small desk. Folding both hands on the desk, he leaned his whole body forward and asked, "Why does a Lebanese Christian boy want to go to a college in Syria?" I tried to explain that there was no way I could attend college in Lebanon because of the civil war. He asked me where I planned to live. I answered that I would rent a room as soon as I could get a job. I asked him if it were possible to work in the college. The chairman did not answer me, and an uncomfortable silence filled the room. He asked if I had friends or relatives in Halab a few moments later. When I told him no, he instantly asked if I knew anyone in Syria. Again I answered no. I mentioned I had met some very nice people while traveling from Beirut to Damascus. The chairman asked if I could prove that my parents would pay for my tuition, room, and food for the four years of college. I was honest and replied that I had very little money and would get a job somewhere in town as soon as I could. He stared at me intensely for a few moments. He got up from his chair and excused himself.

Ten minutes later, he returned with two security men. The two men ordered me to stand up. They tied my hands behind my back, calling me to remain silent. I did not know what was going on. I only knew that I wanted desperately to go to college and become a mathematician or an engineer. I asked the chairman why I was being arrested. He said he thought I was a spy for the Lebanese Christians and only wanted to create trouble in Halab. One of the security men blindfolded me and led me outside to a car. We drove for about ten minutes. Taking me out of the car, they brought me inside a building. I was placed in a chair. They removed the blindfold but left my hands tied.

I found myself surrounded by five Syrian policemen and the two security men. The police officers stood looking very menacing in their black uniforms. Each one wore a pistol around his waist. The security men left the room, leaving me alone with the Syrian Police. One of them asked me the real reason I was in Halab. I told them I only wanted to live and go to school outside Lebanon because Lebanon was a dangerous place to live. I explained that I chose Syria because it was the closest country to Beirut.

Another policeman asked if I were in trouble with the Lebanese government. He said it did not make any sense that a young person would leave his country carrying only a small bag of clothes and no money. He believed I was desperately trying to run away from Lebanon. I said I was desperately trying to avoid the killings and shooting in Lebanon. I had escaped from the war, not from the Lebanese government.

Their interrogation continued, and they asked end-less questions about my family and me. During their grilling, I asked for some food. It had been ages since I had eaten. They exchanged glances and began to laugh hysterically. One of them said they would feed me when I started to admit the truth. I asked how I could be a spy for a government when I had lived in its country for only two months? Just then, the police chief entered the room.

"I was in the other room listening to your answers and watching your body movements. It is simple: if you cooperate with us, we will cooperate with you, but if you play games with us, then we will play games with you."

"I am not playing any games, sir. I swear to Allah I am telling you nothing but the truth," I answered. A silence fell over the men.

The chief scratched his face and asked, "Can you prove you are telling us the truth?" I told them that everything I had said was the truth.

All six men left the room, leaving me alone. I could tell I had been taken to a police station. I did not know why they insisted I was a Lebanese spy. Ten minutes later, the police chief returned with two more police offi-cers. The officer asked me what I thought of the Syrian President, Hafez Assad. I answered that he was the hero of all the Arab nations. The chief seemed pleased with my answer. He asked what I thought of Anwar Al-Sadat, the Egyptian President. I answered that he was a traitor because he planned to make peace with Israel. All three men seemed very happy with my answer, and the chief told me it was great to hear this from a young Lebanese Christian. I added that I had always been against Israel and imperialism. The chief told me he would set me free as long as I promised him I would leave Syria forever.

"I promise and cross my heart that you will never see my face again. I will never enter Syria again as long as I am living!" I shouted excitedly.

The men untied my hands. A few minutes later, the chief offered me a falafel sandwich and a glass of water. I was left alone for a few hours when I finished the sandwich. Three policemen entered and ordered me to go with them in a small Volkswagen. We drove for a few hours, dropping me about two hundred yards from the Lebanese border. They shouted at me to go back to Lebanon and never return to Syria. I arrived close to midnight at the Lebanese army unit stationed between Lebanon and Syria. I was thrilled to be in Lebanon again. I told the Lebanese soldiers stationed at the border about my experience with the Syrian officials. The Lebanese men gave me food, water, and a small bed.

It was early in the morning when one of the Lebanese soldiers awoke me. He told me they would take me home to Antonieh. Coming back like this made me feel like a traitor and a failure. I felt like a traitor because I had run away, leaving my family behind. I felt like a failure because I could not make Syria my new home. Regardless, I was happy to be on my way home. During the trip to Beirut, I realized it was my destiny, written across time, that I should bear witness to the deadly Lebanese civil war.

When I arrived home, I held Mama tightly. She told me she was glad I was okay. The hope I had built up, however, broke into pieces. Going to college had been a dream, but it was a dream I knew I had to pursue one way or another. It seemed like my only choice was to stay in Lebanon and join some Lebanese militia. I grew angry at being barred from Syria because I happened to be Lebanese Christian. I thought life was unfair, yet a small part of me knew I was not ready or willing to give up and die in that war. Cautiously, I nursed this spirit inside me until staying alive and out of battle were the only things important to me.

The civil war in Lebanon escalated daily and covered most of the country. There was an area in the mountains safer than Beirut, but it was too expensive to live there. We slept in our beds less than a dozen times between September and December. Instead, we slept in the hallway. The two walls provided more protection than the single wall in the bedroom. Our hallway was about seven yards long and a yard and a half wide. Once again, most of the neighbors who lived on the floors above us came to our apartment to sleep in the hallway.

There was something comforting about being with other people during heavy and violent shelling. Death did not feel so pressing as it did when we were alone. Sometimes, the people sleeping in our hallway totaled sixteen, including babies. Mama provided mattresses and blankets, never complaining. We had no power in the building for four months because the power plants and lines were damaged. Each family shared their food and water with the rest of the families in the building. If there was only a pound of tomatoes in the building, that pound was equally distributed. Many ovens and stoves in Lebanon had their propane gas container, which mostly kept functioning. The families in the building made sure not to run out of propane gas, with spare supplies stored in the basement of the building.

The women baked bread every day while the men went out to try and retrieve water from springs and creeks and food from any open store in the area. The stores ran out of merchandise many times, so it was a hit-and-miss situation. I used to go out with the men to help gather gallons of water while the fighting continued, and the bullets fell nearby like unwanted stars. I had no idea how I avoided the shooting when I often came close to it. Once we brought back water, it was equally distributed. The four families lived together as one unit, one community. Mama kept three mattresses in the hallway at all times. Those mattresses were the bed for the five of us—my Mama, two sisters, one brother, and me—and some nights, there were additional mattresses for all sixteen residents.

We first had a simple supper of bread and cucumbers or apples whenever the neighbors slept in the hallway.

When vegetables and fruits were not available, we had bread and rice. Bags of flour and rice were stored next to the propane gas cylinders in the basement. After dinner, all the babies and children were put down on one mattress while the adults divided themselves into two groups. One group of four would play bridge. Another group would talk about politics and the war in Lebanon. An adult might have two to three hours of sleep on one of the mattresses. Lying down was impossible, as there was not enough room. Candles were the only source of light and heat. We were hardly cold at night, as the heat of our packed bodies sustained us through the long hours.

During the day, each family stayed in their apartment unless the shelling was severe. In that case, they came down to our apartment area until the shelling subsided. If the shelling did not stop, the neighbors stayed in our hallway for days and nights. This did not often happen, though. Shooting became a normal part of life, so it didn't scare us too much, but the horrible booming sound from the shelling did.

When I did not have to collect spring water with the men, I read Khalil Gibran and math books on the hallway floor. Most of the time, Mama felt ill. She had high blood pressure and diabetes and was beginning to lose vision in one of her eyes. She was always tired from the lack of sleep and poor nutrition. Sometimes I sat next to her, reading from Khalil Gibran. She especially enjoyed our time together because she was illiterate. I think I read the book, *The Prophet*, at least seven times to her. I was sure she memorized it.

She told me that the civil war didn't make sense to anyone. She added that each militia was full of crazy people. She sometimes told me this more than once a day, so I would not become involved in another militia group. Thankfully, no militia had yet come to our house to force Muneer or me to join the fighting. We felt blessed.

There was another cease-fire around Christmas of 1976, and my father came to visit us from Saudi Arabia for two weeks. I so enjoyed spending some little but precious time with him. Those two weeks flew by. Baba returned to Saudi Arabia, and the cease-fire broke at the end of January 1977. Lebanon was once again the playing field of hell. We hardly left the house from January to April. I ran to the store to get rice and flour, the only food items available during those times. Sometimes rice was not attainable, and we ate bread with *zahtar* for weeks at a time. Some stores remained open despite the endless shelling that poured down upon us.

Most of the time, the stores had nothing inside to sell except flour. Bread and flour became so expensive that the price jumped at least ten times over the previous year. The large containers of water were awkward and heavy. Running down the streets of Antonieh, trying to dodge all kinds of explosives, was a living nightmare. Sometimes I was forced to run in a zigzag pattern to avoid being shot at by a sniper. Other times, the bullets were so close I heard the crackle and whistle in my ears like the laughter of the devil's wife. The war in Jordan conducted itself like a lazy Sunday afternoon compared to the civil war that rampaged over Lebanon.

One night in March, the apartment on the fourth floor was hit by a shell. We were sitting in the hallway and could hear the fire burning in the apartment's bedroom. The smoke from the fire made its way into our apartment. All the men went to the fourth floor to fight the fire. We did not want to waste any of our precious water. Some of us went outside the building to dig for soil that we piled upon heavy blankets and carried inside. Dowsing the fire this way took us nearly two hours. Luckily, no one was injured.

9
ESCAPING LEBANON'S CIVIL WAR FOR SPAIN

THE WAR CONTINUED UNTIL MAY 1977, when another cease-fire was called. I was physically, emotionally, and spiritually exhausted and began to think I had to run away again. I thought the best place for me was Kufranja, Jordan, where my oldest sister and her family lived. I thought it would be better to use my Jordanian passport instead of my Lebanese passport. I managed to borrow money from neighbors to pay for the car fare to get to Jordan. I never told my neighbors about my plan; I just told them my family needed the money for daily expenses. Again, I felt guilty about running away, but I was about to lose my life and mind. So, I had no other option but to leave.

I left for Jordan the first week of June 1977 while the latest cease-fire persisted. I ran away while my family was at church. I told them I was not feeling well and wanted to stay home. I left them a similar note to the one I left the previous year and departed for Jordan. This time I was more confident as I had a Jordanian passport and acted like I was going back to my home in Jordan. I took a bus from Beirut to Amman. I wasn't harassed in Syria at all this time, as my destination was Jordan and not Halab. The trip from Beirut to Jordan was long but went smoothly. During the ten-hour ride, I felt like a deserter escaping the horrific war by myself.

Aida, her husband, and their five children were shocked but happy when I arrived at their home in Kufranja.

Kufranja was a tiny town, smaller than Mafraq. I could not find a job and was broke and bored two weeks after my arrival. I had no way to call my Mama to tell her I was safe with Aida, as the communication lines in Lebanon were destroyed due to the conflict.

I decided to go to Spain to work and attend college. I heard from Aida's neighbors that it was easier to obtain a visa to get there than to other European countries. I had to go to Amman, the capital of Jordan, to obtain a visa from the Spanish Embassy. They gave me a visitor's visa to be in Spain for months. I went directly to Mafraq as soon as I obtained the visa and borrowed money from old friends to buy the airline ticket to fly from Amman to Madrid. After buying my ticket, I was left with around fifty dollars. When I went back to Kufranja to tell Aida and her family about my good news, they weren't thrilled about me going to Spain to attend college. They were worried, but I was determined to leave all the bloody strife in the Middle East.

In early July 1977, I flew from Jordan to Spain. It was my first time flying. The trip from Amman to Madrid felt like it lasted forever. I had no idea what Spain looked like or what the people might be like. All I had was a backpack, which contained a couple of pants, shirts, three pairs of underwear, and a couple of socks.

I didn't speak Spanish, but I managed to get to downtown Madrid. Train stations were spotless and organized. I had never ridden a train before, so everything was foreign to me. Madrid was huge, too busy, and crowded. It was challenging to ask people for directions to the parks. I planned to make them my new home since I would spend my nights there. I knew I wouldn't be able to afford to stay in hotels or even hostels, for that matter. I lived in one of the parks for several days before I was discovered by someone who asked me to leave. Finding food was somewhat challenging. Sometimes I asked people to give me food; most of them were kind enough to share their food. Some tried to talk to me, but I had no idea what they were saying. I am sure a few thought I was mentally challenged, but that didn't bother me. I kept smiling at them while they tried to open a conversation. The exchanges didn't last long after they found out I couldn't respond to them.

I had been in Madrid for a week without making progress in my job search. I felt fortunate, though, to meet two Egyptian men in the city who counseled me to travel to southern Spain, Andalusia – a region filled with Arab people. They also gave me a Spanish-Arabic dictionary. My hitchhiking trek started in Madrid and took me to Seville, Cadiz, Malaga, and Granada. Along the way, I began learning rudimentary Spanish by using my dictionary and reading old newspapers I found in the trash, on park benches, or at bus stops. I was forced to speak to Spanish residents who helped me with pronunciation and vocabulary. It was fun trying to talk to and make friends with them. However, it was tough for me to find people my age, as most folks I encountered in the parks were much older. I guessed people my age were in school and college during the day. At night, I slept in church parking lots or on park benches.

Despite walking the streets of each city searching for any kind of job, I hit a brick wall. I had been in Spain for three weeks, and while each city had its special charms, I began to despair. I was always scared and worried in the dark when alone, sleeping in the open.

When I reached Malaga, I met several Arab people who told me to go to Granada. They said there was not only a large Arab community, but the college there was excellent, and the people were friendly. I threw my frayed brown canvas bag containing my few belongings over my shoulder and hitchhiked to Granada, hoping for better fortune.

Once I arrived in Granada, I instantly fell in love with the city. The old part of Granada was beautiful.

I was welcomed with a brilliant blue sky and scorching warmth from the sun on my first day. Granada, at the time, was well known as a student city. Many of its population came from around the world to study at its universities and colleges. There were tourists everywhere. I enjoyed watching crowds pass by while I sat at a bus stop or in the park.

Spain had been host to Arabic culture for centuries, which I felt in my core. Walking along the streets of Granada, I was overcome by the city's magic. Granada sits at the point where the Sierra Nevada Mountains meet the fertile plain of the Vega. From a distance, I was able to see craggy mountains rising above the flat agricultural land. I visited some monolithic churches and museums. Alhambra, a massive castle constructed over many centuries, was located in Granada. It consisted of gardens, fortifications, and sumptuous rooms. It had been the home to many Arabic sultans who had ruled the whole province of Granada.

Albaicin, the old Arabic quarter, was located on the hill opposite the Alhambra. Cobble-stoned streets and whitewashed houses characterized it. The Albaicin was an oil painter's paradise, and almost every turn of the head produced a beautiful view.

As I walked along the streets of Granada, I noticed that Spanish women looked very similar to Lebanese women with their brunette hair, dark-colored eyes, olive complexion, and voluptuous-shaped bodies. It drove me crazy to see Spanish women wearing tight pants and low-cut blouses. I kept telling myself to stop staring but was so fascinated by them that I couldn't help myself. I lusted after them. I wanted a woman; any woman would do for me. Because I was living on the streets, no woman noticed me.

I kept working at learning Spanish on my own, and talking to passersby about directions, just to open a conversation with someone. I managed to eat leftovers on the street, and trash containers always had uneaten food. For the most part, it all tasted great to a hungry teenager. Many times I thought of my family, especially my Mama. I missed them all terribly; however, I knew I had made the right decision deep inside.

I looked for jobs everywhere around the city. I asked at bars if I could clean the floors and the bathrooms for a small wage, but nobody wanted to hire me. Some did feed me, though. I sometimes even knocked at people's houses and asked if I could clean their houses, but all I received were rejections. I didn't mind the rejections as long as they gave me a piece of bread or some fruits to eat. When I asked for work at a small store, they gave me a sandwich after politely kicking me out. Everything started to look dark around me. Many times, I had to beg for a piece of bread. Yet, I felt it was safer than being in the civil war in Lebanon. So, every time I felt like a failure in Spain, I thought about the bullets and shelling in Beirut, which provided much comfort.

One day, I tried finding a job in a fancy-looking hotel. I entered the lobby and was amazed by the smooth marble, ornate architecture, exotic-looking people, and the intoxicating smell of food. This last thing overwhelmed me. I wished smelling the food was enough to fill me up.

An older man who worked at the hotel approached me. He asked if I needed help. I told him I needed a job. The gentleman frowned. He accompanied me to the main door and told me to leave. I continued walking further down the street when I came upon a supermarket.

I stood in line as if I were a shopper. When my turn came, I told the cashier I needed a job. She called the manager. I was excited to meet him. He took me by the arm and escorted me outside. I saw a gas station with a little store attached to the building. I asked the man inside if I could work for him. He asked me if I knew anything about cars. I told him I didn't. He asked me if I had a driver's license. I was naïve and honest. I told him the only thing I had ever driven was a camel and a horse. He kicked me out.

I walked down the street and noticed a small grocery store. It was crowded with customers. Two women stood behind the counter; one seemed to be in her late fifties, the other in her mid-thirties. They looked like they might be mother and daughter. The two women hardly noticed me because they were busy helping customers. One of them cut ham while the other woman ran the cash register. I felt a stabbing pain in my stomach when I saw the ham, cheese, apples, and food everywhere. I wanted to eat all of it. I avoided making eye contact with either woman because I did not want them to throw me out. Finally, the older woman noticed me and said, "Hey you, how can I help you?"

In a low faltering voice with my broken Spanish, I replied, "I'm looking for a job, but please don't kick me out." She didn't understand what I was saying. The young lady next to her stopped cutting the ham and examined me. I stared at both of them, appealing to the older woman with my eyes to not throw me out but to give me a job.

She asked me what kind of job I was looking for. I told her I would do anything. I said I would work for food and a room; that's all I wanted. "You don't need to pay me; just feed me and give me a room," I emphasized.

The young lady said, "What, do you mean you don't want to be paid?"

I repeated that I just wanted food and a room. The older woman asked if I could drive a truck. I told her I couldn't. She said she needed someone to drive a truck to deliver goods to the store. I told her I could unload the truck. She said she didn't have a room, but she could feed me. She said she only needed me to work for three hours a day. I asked her if I could start now. The young lady said the truck wasn't there yet. I asked her when the truck would arrive. The two women fell silent for a moment. Finally, the older woman told me to wait while she finished with the customers.

I waited desperately for her to come back and talk with me. The older woman showed me the storage area in the back of the building. A large freezer made the room cold, but I didn't care. A long hallway ran the length of the room. It was filled with wine, beer, soda, and canned foods. Legs of ham dangled from the ceiling, which was torture for me as I had been hungry for days. She showed me where the goods were stored, and on which shelves they were stacked. I said the hallway was dirty and offered to sweep. It wasn't that dirty, but I had to lie in order to get a job. The older woman became angry, asking me if I was criticizing her neatness. I apologized, telling her I thought she might give me an apple to eat if I swept the floor. She asked about my family. She wanted to know where I was from and what I was doing in Spain. I told her the truth: I was just a Lebanese boy escaping the civil war.

She said it was a tragedy about what was happening in Lebanon. She told me to stay in the warehouse, and she would be right back. A few minutes later, she returned with a key, unlocked the warehouse's back door, and took me outside to the unpaved parking lot. My heart sunk as I thought she might be kicking me out. Instead, she took me behind the building and showed me empty boxes strewn over the parking area. She ordered me to collect all the boxes and stack them neatly. I was so happy to have a job I wanted to kiss her. The only thing that stopped me was the fear if I kissed her, I would lose my job before officially getting it. Just as I started to collect the boxes, the woman gave me an apple and a banana to eat first. She watched me shove the banana and apple down my mouth.

I brought the boxes to the warehouse and stacked them the way the woman instructed. On my third trip back to the warehouse, my hands full of boxes, I spied the older woman waiting for me with a ham and cheese sandwich and a big glass of water. I took the sandwich from her and eagerly ate it. I don't remember if I even chewed it.

After finishing the sandwich and water, I returned to bring over more boxes. Again, the older woman met me in the warehouse with another sandwich. I ate the second sandwich. She asked me if I wanted something else to eat. She was shocked when I said yes, indeed. She inquired when I had last eaten. I told her it wasn't too long ago. She laughed and said if she hired me for meals, I would surely break her. I went back to my task as she left to get something else for me to eat.

When I came back to the warehouse, the young lady waited for me this time. She had a bottle of Pepsi and another ham and cheese sandwich. Though she was reticent, her eyes were very expressive. They raked me over from head to toe. She was much older than me, and I wished she were my age. I ate my sandwich in silence. I felt uncomfortable and thought she wanted to go back to the store. The older woman broke our silence when she returned to the warehouse. She asked if I was still hungry.

"No, ma'am, thank you. Thank you so much."

The young woman asked where I lived. I told her I didn't live anywhere now; I had no place to stay. The older woman wondered if I had any clothes. I told her my clothes were inside the brown bag I left outside her store door. The older woman asked if I minded staying overnight in the warehouse; if it would be too cold. I eagerly accepted the offer, telling her it wouldn't be too cold. The older woman told me her name was Esther, and the younger woman's name was Katia.

Both ladies expressed satisfaction with how I stacked the boxes in the warehouse. I noticed Katia's long, silky, dark hair that fell to her lower back. Her black, wide eyes reminded me of Bedouins' eyes, and I couldn't help noticing her voluptuous bosom. She was on the heavy side but healthy and beautiful. I did my best to avoid looking at her chest. I did not want the two women to look at my pants. I wondered if Katia were married or single. My mind drifted, and I imagined her naked while Esther asked me if I wanted to pick up my clothes from outside the store and bring them inside the warehouse. I asked Esther if I could work more than three hours a day, which she had suggested earlier. I wanted to work as long as the store was open. Katia asked me if longer hours included being paid in meals and board. I nodded. She said, "It's a deal."

Esther told me they had an old mattress for me to sleep on in the warehouse, which made me happy I would not have to sleep on the cold concrete. She said the grocery store opened from nine in the morning until one in the afternoon, closed at one, and reopened from three to nine o'clock. The store stayed open daily except for Sundays. Katia added I would not be allowed behind the cash register or in the grocery store without their permission. My main job was working in the warehouse and cleaning and sweeping outside the store, including the sidewalk. I would also unload the truck when the delivery came, move boxes from the warehouse to the store, and collect trash from the store and the warehouse.

Esther told me that each time I ate or drank anything from the store, I needed to report it in a notebook she would provide, including each meal's date and time. I was so excited I had gotten this job and felt relieved I wouldn't have any more hunger pains. Both ladies informed me they were going home at one o'clock and would be back to reopen the store at three. They instructed me to stay in the warehouse to wait for the truck, which was supposed to arrive at any moment. They explained where all the goods were kept and how to stack them.

I watched them leave, lock the store's main door behind them, and cross the street to the high-rise building where they lived. I sat on the warehouse floor, looking at the endless array of food and soda. I felt like I was in the middle of a dream. Just then, I heard the rumble of the delivery truck. The driver directed me to unload the goods from the truck. The job went smoothly, and I began to enjoy it. I felt responsible, capable, and necessary. It was just before three o'clock when the truck pulled away. A few minutes later, I heard the main door of the grocery shop open. The two women entered the warehouse, inspecting my job. They both smiled, satisfied.

Within minutes, customers began filtering into the store, keeping the women very busy. I tried to keep myself occupied in the warehouse. Around seven that evening, I was sweeping outside of the store when Katia came to ask if I were hungry.

"I'm always hungry, ma'am."

She laughed.

"What do you do with all this food? Why are you so damn skinny? Take a look at me, every time I eat a sandwich, it sticks to me. I am fat. I am more than ten kilograms overweight."

I interrupted her, saying, "You are not fat. You are a beautiful, healthy woman."

Her face blushed a telling crimson. I apologized right away, saying I did not mean to make her feel uncomfortable.

"No, it wasn't your fault," she said. "I am just not used to a man complimenting me. Especially a young man like you."

"Forgive me for being rude, but any man would be lucky to marry you."

This made her laugh loudly. When she spoke again, her voice was calm. "I'm already married. But my husband, Pedro, doesn't feel too lucky."

"Unless your husband is blind, he should know how fortunate he is."

She said, "Let's go back to the food. What do you want to eat?"

"Anything you want to make me, Katia, would be great," I responded.

She walked towards the door. My eyes hugged her back, fixated on her firm, round behind. Before she got to the grocery store door, she turned to face me. We stared at each other for a moment, and then she was gone. I continued to sweep, feeling disappointed she was married.

A few minutes later, she returned with two sandwiches, an apple, and a big water bottle. She told me to wash my hands in the small bathroom in the warehouse before I touched the food. I did as she asked. When I returned, I asked if she had any children. She laughed and said she had no time. Then I asked if she was a newlywed. She smiled and said she had been married for twelve years.

"Any more questions?"

I looked back at her silently.

Then she said, "For every question, you ask me, I will ask you two. Do we have a deal here?" Before I answered her, she smiled and walked toward the store.

The store was empty, and as I ate my sandwich and apple, I couldn't help overhearing Esther and Katia shouting at each other. I thought how foolish it was for a mother and daughter to argue that way.

I made my way back to the warehouse and busied myself with anything just to be away from them. Esther followed behind me a few minutes later, saying Katia was stubborn and stupid. I did not respond. Esther continued, saying Katia was selfish and lazy. While the older woman spoke, Katia walked into the warehouse. She signaled behind Esther with her finger, indicating the older woman was crazy.

I told Esther, "I hope I did not create any problem between you and Katia." She said it wasn't me; it was Katia, as always. I went outside the store to finish sweeping the sidewalk. A few minutes later, when Katia came outside to check my work, I asked her softly why she fought with her mother. I told her she should love and respect her mom. She said, "I do. I do. But that bitch is not my mother; she is my mother-in-law."

"She's Pedro's mother."

"Where is Pedro now?" I asked. "Does he work here as well?"

"No," she said. "He has his own bakery downtown. You'll meet him tonight when he brings you the mattress."

"Do you and Pedro live with her in the same apartment?"

Katia rolled her eyes. "Yes," she said. She excused herself to go back to the store.

It was about nine o'clock when Katia and Esther left the store. Before they stepped outside, they reminded me that Pedro would be back soon with the mattress and pillow. I was happy to hear that. It gave me hope that they were hiring me to work for them. They made sure the door was locked behind them, and I watched as they walked along the street. I could tell from how they moved their hands emphatically at each other that they were still arguing. Staring at the way Katia walked, the way her body performed its sensual dance beneath her clothes, made me want to go to the bathroom and masturbate. Katia was much bigger than me; if I ever hugged her, my body could easily get lost in her.

An hour later, I heard the front door of the store open. Katia walked in with a man in his forties, short with a big belly, almost like Buddha. His round face was covered with a reddish beard, and he was partially bald. His head's thin, red hair ran as straight as a ruler. The man scrutinized me, eyeing every inch of my body, just like Katia did when she first met me.

Katia said, "The mattress is in the lobby of our building so you and Pedro can go pick it up."

I stretched out my arm to shake hands with Pedro. "You must be Katia's husband. It is a pleasure to meet you."

Pedro coldly shook my hand, hardly saying a word, but I could smell alcohol on his breath. We crossed the street towards the building. Katia walked ahead to open the door for us. The mattress stood against the far wall of the lobby. Pedro and I carried the mattress while Katia held the door open. Pedro led the way, and as I walked past Katia, she pulled towards me, causing my left elbow to brush against her big, sexy breast. I wasn't sure if she did that intentionally or accidentally. Regardless, I whispered, "I'm sorry." She acted like she didn't notice me. However, her face turned to flame. Pedro did not notice.

Once we placed the mattress, the three of us made up the bed with sheets. I noticed an even more pungent scent of alcohol coming from Pedro's mouth. I asked Katia if she had been able to find a blanket and pillow. She looked at me and said, "Oh, I forgot them," with a sheepish smile. "I'll be back later with them."

Once Pedro and Katia were finished helping me, they turned to leave. Pedro asked me before she locked the door behind them, "So, you're Lebanese. Are you Muslim?"

"No, I'm Christian."

"For real? I didn't know there were Christians in Lebanon."

"Sure, there are," I said.

Katia chimed in, "What kind?"

I said, "I'm Catholic."

She said excitedly, "You're Catholic? So am I. I mean, so are we."

Bidding me goodnight, they crossed the street to their apartment. Pedro stumbled along the road beside Katia.

I waited for more than an hour for Katia to return with my pillow and blanket. I was so tired, I decided to sleep without a pillow or a cover. It was mid-October, and here it was my first night having a mattress under me for a long time. I felt like a human being again. The warehouse was unbelievably cold. Despite sleeping in all my clothes, I still froze. I missed the bed in my brother's room and hated being alone.

I tossed and turned most of the night. Every noise from the refrigerators, freezers or passing cars made me jumpy. My mind drifted to other places, and the picture of Katia's breasts came before me. I imagined my face buried in her cleavage. I fantasized about her in a sweater and pants that were tight enough to show the curves of her body. My thoughts made me horny again, but I was too lazy, tired, and cold to get up to the bathroom to masturbate.

It was almost midnight when I heard someone trying to open the store's front door. I got up from the mattress so quickly that I almost lost my balance. I hurried to the light switch and nervously gave it a flick. I was relieved to see Katia carrying a pillow and a couple of blankets. My crotch was still enlarged and ready to burst through my pants. Thinking about her had made me very excited, but seeing her was different. She was suddenly real, in front of me. My heart pounded the way it had long ago when Israeli pilots attacked me. But this time, I was being attacked by a Spanish woman who made me hard each time I looked at her.

She said warmly, "Here are the pillow and blankets I promised." I couldn't respond. I felt too scared to walk toward her to take the blankets and pillow and couldn't even stretch my arms in her direction.

"Sorry I came a little late," she said. "I hope I wasn't interrupting anything. Did I wake you up? Were you sleeping?"

"No, I wasn't," I said. "I was just waiting for you."

"Waiting for me? What do you mean?"

"Oh nothing, I meant I was waiting for the pillow," I said. "Somehow, I thought you would bring me the pillow and blankets right after you left with Pedro."

She apologized for coming late, explaining she had to make dinner for Pedro. She said she showered and came here as soon as she finished. I asked her if Pedro was waiting. After she finished her shower, she told me, Pedro was already in bed, fast asleep. She disclosed he usually went to bed by eleven-thirty, while she retired at around one in the morning. I asked her why she went to bed so late. Katia answered that she napped in the afternoon when the store closed. She told me Pedro never closed his bakery for a siesta, and, as a result, he came home exhausted each night, wanting only his whisky and dinner. I asked what she did in the hours before her bedtime. Katia said rather sadly she either watched TV, read, or knitted. Esther, she added, also went to bed by ten-thirty each evening.

Katia reminded me of what she told me earlier; she would ask me two for every question I asked her. She surprised me, and I didn't know how to respond. Clearing my throat, I said I was only curious. I added she could ask me any question she wanted, but I might bore her with my answers. She said she doubted that, handed me the pillow and blankets, and said she better go. I apologized for asking too many questions and explained that I didn't have friends here and was sometimes lonely. She told me not to worry as she understood the meaning of loneliness well. She waved back at me as she crossed the street.

I went to my mattress, covered myself with the blankets, and rolled right and left all night thinking about Katia's body. I felt that night, since I had a mattress, I would sleep all night, but sadly it didn't work that way.

I rose at about eight o'clock the following day. I washed my face in the little bathroom, ate cheese and bread, and put my mattress out of the way. Just before nine, the store door opened, and the two ladies entered. Katia made sure I wrote down what I ate and drank for breakfast.

Esther ordered Katia and me to stock the store. She told us to go to the storage room and pick up as many items as we could to stock the shelves completely. I followed Katia to the warehouse and picked up materials she pointed at on the high ceiling shelves and took them inside the store. When I returned from the store to the warehouse, I saw Katia on a step ladder trying to collect items from the shelves. I ran towards her to help ensure she didn't trip over the boxes. However, she caught me several times looking at her in profound thought. Each time I turned my face away. In the meantime, I also caught Katia's eyes trained on me as if they were going through me. One day inside the warehouse, when Katia and I were all alone, she asked me, "Why are you looking at me this way? Or is this my imagination?"

I lowered my head and didn't say a word. She told me she wasn't used to having a man look at her the way I did. I kept silent, my head still down, staring at the warehouse floor.

Katia continued, "I am not upset; actually, I am thrilled that a young man would look at me and think I'm an attractive woman."

In a quiet voice, I said, "I didn't mean any harm by looking at you. Even God loves beautiful things. Nothing is wrong with being beautiful. This red dress you have on fits you perfectly and makes you look like a model. Pedro is crazy not to notice you."

She smiled faintly and said Pedro was forty, not a teenager like me. She asked me how old I was and when I told her I was eighteen, she laughed, saying she was fifteen years older than me. She told me to find a girl my age, as she was too fat and old for me. I told her I liked her sexy body.

"Stop," she told me with a smile. "You are embarrassing me!"

She ran to the store and left me alone in the storage room. I wasn't sure if I had really embarrassed her or made her feel good. Shortly after the two ladies got settled for the day, customers began to stream in. I went on to do my work and was outside for about two hours, sweeping and cleaning, when Esther asked me to help carry boxes of potatoes from the warehouse to the store. She directed me to display the potatoes neatly in their designated area. Esther asked Katia to help me since the store wasn't that busy. I stood very close to Katia as we worked. Her scent was clean and fresh, like mountain flowers despite the dry, dusty city. I wanted to sniff her like a dog sniffs a piece of meat. I tried to get closer and touch the arm that unloaded the potatoes onto the shelf like a machine. I couldn't help tilting my head to sniff her luxurious hair. She looked at me now and then with a smile. I wasn't sure if she had noticed that I was trying to smell her. She finally whispered in my ear to stop. She said if Esther saw me she would fire me, and I would be hungry and homeless again. I whispered back and told her I liked her perfume. She chuckled and said she would buy me a perfume bottle to smell if that were all. I told her it was not only the perfume that drove me wild. She laughed again and said I was a lunatic but brave. I apologized for my aggressive nose. She said there was nothing I needed to apologize for. The day ended fast. It was nine o'clock before I knew it, and both ladies left, locking the door behind them.

Two weeks after I started working for the two ladies, Esther allowed me to go to their apartment every Friday night to take a shower. I always tried to make my shower time after 11:30 PM on Friday when Esther and Pedro were already sleeping. Sometimes, both ladies bought me clothes on alternate Sundays. They also gave me a toothbrush and toothpaste. It was a new ritual that

182

fascinated me. I did not like the way my gums bled now and then, but I did notice the difference in the color of my teeth as I brushed them between four to five times a day. Because it was a novelty, I thoroughly enjoyed it.

My bosses treated me as if I was a part of their family. Esther insisted on paying me some little money every Saturday, besides supplying the food and the mattress, and the weekly shower. Also, every other Sunday, the ladies invited me to have dinner with them and Pedro in their three-bedroom apartment. There was often tension in the house between Katia and Pedro, Katia and Esther, or sometimes even between Esther and Pedro. I also noticed that Katia and Pedro hardly talked to each other. And Pedro hardly ever spoke to me. Pedro would speak with his mother, Esther, occasionally but not often. Pedro was a quiet man but a heavy drinker. I was not fond of the alternate Sundays when I did not share dinner with my bosses, as the store was closed and locked, and sometimes I spent that whole day and night by myself in the store and warehouse.

Around three months after I was hired, Esther ordered Katia and me to organize the vegetable table. So, Katia and I stood next to each other, removing the old and rotten vegetables from the display table. Again, I began smelling her, and now and then, our arms rubbed against each other accidentally. We traded smiles. I was worried Esther would notice and throw me out on the streets again.

After Katia and I finished our assignment, Esther

asked us to bring more potatoes into the store. Katia asked me if I liked her perfume today. I didn't know where I got the courage when I told her it wasn't only her perfume driving me crazy. Without hesitation, Katia asked me what else was driving me crazy. I said in a very low voice that her body was. She told me she wished her husband would give her as many compliments as I did. Then I asked her when her husband last complimented her. She stared in thought at the potatoes and said she couldn't remember.

I asked if she would be kind enough to hug me, but she claimed it was inappropriate. I asked her when it would be appropriate to give me a simple hug. I hardly finished my sentence when she said right now. We stood by the potato boxes in the warehouse; Katia stared into my eyes as if she wanted to eat them. She threw her arms around my neck. I grabbed her waist and pulled her towards me. My arms enveloped her back, making her body touch and rub against mine. I heard her breathing quicken. She captured her lips between mine, and we started kissing.

She took my tongue on a journey inside her mouth. I rubbed up hungrily against her. My crotch was about to explode from my pants. I kissed her over and over. She asked me to stop, saying Esther might be looking for us. She told me we would both be in significant trouble if Esther saw us. I stopped and let go of her. I picked up a box of potatoes and handed it to her. I took her face between my palms and kissed her again as she held the box. She told me to clean the red lipstick off my lips and disappeared from the warehouse. I wiped my lips and, taking another box, I followed her to the front. Esther was still occupied with customers. I casually passed by and resumed helping Katia with the display.

Katia and I kept our distance the rest of the afternoon. I was up for most of the night. I couldn't wait for the morning to arrive so I could see Katia. Finally, my two bosses opened the store. Katia asked me to follow her to the warehouse as she had something for me to do. Once we were alone in the warehouse, Katia told me that she had felt happy and confident ever since I started paying attention to her. She said she wished Pedro would hug and kiss her as he used to in the past. She complained that Pedro hadn't been romantic with her or made love to her for a long time. For the last few years, when Pedro came home, the first thing he did was hug his whisky bottle and kiss his whisky glass. She said the only thing her husband made love to was his cigarettes. Katia asked me how she could feel like a woman when she didn't even feel like there was a man in her life.

I kept reminding her she was gorgeous.

Katia interrupted me and said, "I bet you hit on every woman you see. Tell me how many girlfriends you have? How many women have you slept with?"

I told her I had never kissed a woman or had sex before. She said I was pushing my luck with an old, fat woman. I reminded her, again, that she wasn't fat or old.

"You don't think I am old and fat?"

I responded if I didn't think she was beautiful, how could I be so aroused when I kissed her and held her the day before? I asked her if she felt my penis against her body in the warehouse when we hugged and kissed. She didn't reply.

I said, "I guess it was too small for you to feel."

She replied, "It was huge, like a hammer."

She started to laugh loudly. I took one of her hands, held it between my own for a few moments, and began to kiss it. She was watching me like a hunter watching his prey. Slowly, she pulled her hand away, lowered it, and placed it on my penis. She explored my pants on her own. Katia began massaging my penis through my pants. I was getting harder and harder, and what she was doing felt so good I wanted to open my pants. She wouldn't let me. I felt like my penis could stretch up to touch the warehouse ceiling when Esther shouted and said she needed our help. Katia and I ran into the store to help Esther and acted as if nothing had happened.

10
RETURNING TO WAR-TORN LEBANON

SUNDAY, MY DAY OFF, was always a long day for me. I was basically in an isolated teenage jail. I thought about my family in Lebanon – were they dead or alive? I often wished I was back in Lebanon in the hallway with my family and neighbors. At least I would have people to talk with, and in Arabic, my first language. I missed reading Khalil Gibran to Mama. I yearned to sleep with four or five adults on one mattress. I didn't know anything about loneliness there. I wanted to go back home to touch people. I missed hugging them, kissing them, and joking with them. I reminded myself that I came to Spain to study math or physics, as I was planning to become an engineer one day, and not to be inside a warehouse seven days a week, 24 hours a day. However, at this point, Lebanon was still on fire, and I was concerned about going back and having to join a militia group.

Otherwise, my time in Granada continued as before. I unloaded trucks, swept the warehouse and sidewalk, and organized merchandise. My relationship with Katia went on - in the warehouse during the work-week and in her apartment on Friday nights. We stole moments together whenever we could. Katia, however, did not want to go all the way, as she was afraid of getting pregnant. I respected her wishes even though I wanted to feel what it was like to have sex.

In late May, Esther walked in on Katia and me while in the warehouse making out. Esther yelled out that Katia was the biggest whore in town. She then turned to me and barked that we were both cheap empty shells. She shouted that I used to be homeless and starving. She had fed me and given me a place to live, and I took advantage of her, her son, and her daughter-in-law, who was as immoral as I. I started to cry. I wished the ground would open up and swallow me. I apologized to Esther. She interrupted me by saying bastards like me never apologized sincerely. She continued to say I had destroyed her son's life and Katia's life. She said she should have never hired me. Katia and I both burst into tears. Katia remained silent during the whole episode while I apologized to Esther. Esther interrupted me by saying she had suspected something for a while. I tried telling Esther this would never happen again, but she screamed at me to shut up. She wanted me out of the store immediately and told me to come back the follow-ing Monday to pick up my train ticket to Madrid and airplane ticket from Madrid to Beirut. I begged her to give me another chance, but she told me she had already given me a chance, and I shit on it.

I collected all my clothes and left the store for my old home, the streets and parks of Granada. Thankfully, I made some money to buy food until the next Monday when I went to the store to collect my tickets. Katia was cutting ham as usual, and Esther was behind the register. Katia didn't look at me while Esther gave me the tickets. I tried to talk to Esther, but she interrupted me, saying if I didn't leave right away, she planned to call the police. Unlike a family member or an employee, I left the store a perfect stranger, tears rolling down my face.

I took the train to Madrid that night, feeling empty. I cried on the train as if I were a baby looking for his mommy. Once I arrived at the Madrid airport, I felt stronger and more determined to go home and enroll in college, one way or another. However, I didn't know if my family was alive, injured, or even dead. I wasn't sure what I would find when I arrived in Beirut.

In the coming months, I realized that my relationship with Katia was based solely on animal lust, fueled by loneliness. Being confined to the warehouse had made me crave human touch and want to be seen as a human being. While I concluded that neither Katia nor the warehouse was my future, I felt guilty and ashamed about what happened between me, Katia, and Esther.

It was late May 1977. I was fortunate to arrive in Beirut during a cease-fire. When I returned home,

Mama nearly fainted from happiness. She told me she had been sick with worry, primarily when she had not heard a word from me while I was gone. Baba was still in Saudi Arabia, and my two sisters and brother were thrilled to see me alive.

My family told me the situation in Lebanon had been improving, getting safer, only to find out several days later that they were wrong. In just those few days, Beirut was burning again—the shelling, snipers, machine-gun fire, and bombs exploding very close to home. The war intensified until September 1977, when another cease-fire was declared.

When the cease-fire was announced, the first thing I decided to do was register at the Lebanese University and major in physics. I wanted to major in engineering as this was my dream, but since the college did not offer this program, I decided physics was my second best option. The Lebanese University was only fifteen minutes walking distance from my home. I loved the college, even though I was one of the few Christian students. The university was located in the west Beirut sector. Beirut was divided into two separate sections, east, and west. My family lived in the eastern sector, where Christians resided, but my college was located in West Beirut, where the Muslims lived. Since the Lebanese were being killed based on their religion, every time I crossed from the Christian to the Muslim sector, my life hung by a thread. Mama always worried about me crossing over "the life and death line," as the Lebanese people named it, since you could be shot from either side of the fence. I, however, was determined to continue attending university.

The university employed a French system where students attended classes for nine months. After nine months, they had one test for each of their classes. If the student passed the exam, they would be able to register for the second year of classes. If the student did not pass the exam, they would have to repeat the entire first year.

Three weeks after I enrolled in the Lebanese University, Beirut turned savage. The civil war raged with the Palestinian guerrillas and the Lebanese Muslim militia allied against the Lebanese Christian militia. Schools and universities were closed as the civil war continued to escalate. I missed more than six weeks of school before another cease-fire was finally declared. My sister, Sonia, was supposed to get married at Christmas, but she and her fiancé decided to get married earlier during the cease-fire. The wedding was beautiful but quick and very simple. My college reopened for three weeks before the civil war in Lebanon heated up once again.

In the first week of February 1978, I walked with a friend in West Beirut during another cease-fire period when we approached the U.S. Embassy. A sign written in English hung outside the Embassy building. I didn't know English, so I decided to go in and ask somebody what the sign meant. My friend thought I was crazy. He told me the American guard might arrest me. I asked him to come in with me, but he refused, thinking my idea was irrational.

My palms began to sweat as I entered the Embassy. I almost turned back when one of the guards asked me what I wanted. I asked him in Arabic about the sign. The man didn't understand me. He escorted me to the receptionist and then a clerk, who spoke some Arabic. She told me they were accepting applications from Lebanese students to go to the U.S. to study. I asked her how many students they were taking. Her blue eyes were fixed on me, seeing through me. After a moment, she smiled and said maybe 100 students or maybe 50. I asked how many students had applied. She took a deep breath and said she wasn't sure, but she guessed several thousand. I looked at her and asked her what chance I had for my application to be accepted. Opening her drawer, she said she didn't know and passed me an application form. She said if I filled it out, she was sure I had a better chance of being accepted than if I didn't.

I asked her if she would mind helping me fill out the application. She studied me and said I should take the application with me and fill it out at my own pace at home. I repeated my request. Again, she looked at me suspiciously and took another deep breath, saying I was too persistent.

Taking out a pen, she started to help me fill out the application. After we finished, she instructed me to return with my transcript from the university I currently attended. On the way home, I told myself, "Isn't it ironic I used to shout, 'Death to America,' as a young boy on the streets of Mafraq, and here I am applying to

American Universities to study and escape Lebanon's civil war." After all, I reminded myself that America was the best and most advanced country in the world.

In five days, I returned with the materials she'd asked for. I was impressed that she recognized me. As soon as she saw me, she grinned and said, "Oh no, you again?" I smiled back and told her I had looked forward to giving her my transcript. She asked me with her heavy Arabic accent if I was anxious about going to America. I told her I wasn't; I had wanted to come back to the embassy to see her beautiful face once more. She laughed so hard that her cheeks became red. Collecting my transcripts, she asked what my major was. I told her physics, and she smiled again, saying I didn't look like a physics guy to her. I thanked her for the compliment even though I didn't understand it.

"In America, I want to study engineering," I told the enchanting clerk. She reviewed my transcript and then asked what kind of engineering I wanted to study in the U.S. I told her civil, as I loved to build things. She nodded cheerfully and asked me to sit and wait for an interview.

The interview lasted a few minutes. I was asked if I had ever traveled to any countries outside Lebanon. When I answered "Yes," they asked me to list them and how long I stayed in each country. The interviewer asked what I was doing in Spain, and I replied I had worked there. He inquired how I managed to live in Spain without knowing the language.

"It is the same way some U.S. embassy employees manage to live here without knowing Arabic," I answered.

I kept my visit to the U.S. Embassy a secret from my family. I didn't want to give them false hope. I knew deep inside I had no chance of going, as many students had already applied before me. Again, the university closed as the war was out of control. Bombs careened down in Beirut, and our neighbors moved into our hallway again. It was like déjà vu. Some people played cards, and others laid down on the mattresses. Mama prayed to Allah with her rosaries. I heard her ask Allah to keep the bombs away from our hallway. I heard her order Him to stop the deadly civil war. My sister declared she wished we had never left Jordan. In the distance, children shouted they didn't want to die.

Listening to the cacophony of screaming, crying children, and murmuring adults made me think I was stupid for what I did with Katia, causing me to be kicked out of Spain. Even though I had been lonely, at least I had been safe. The fighting in Lebanon went on sporadically. One week showers of bombs and bullets were relentless, and the following week nothing but a few snipers disturbed the air. I became so used to it that I joked with Mama before I went to bed that if there weren't any bombings or shootings, I wouldn't be able to sleep; it would be too quiet.

We all lived this way until December 1978. The college I attended rarely opened as the fighting in the streets continued. Our hallway was often filled with neighbors. The second week of December, my Baba came to visit us from Saudi Arabia to spend Christmas. He said he had five weeks of vacation. His plane landed in Beirut in the early evening. I decided to meet him at the airport even though I knew it was dangerous. The airport was in West Beirut, where the Lebanese Muslims and Palestinians lived. As a young Lebanese Christian man, I was an easy target.

There was some gunfire on the way to the airport, but nothing I couldn't handle. I saw Baba coming quickly towards me. He was scared when he heard the shooting. I calmed him and said the shooting was not dangerous. I explained as long as we didn't have bombs or shells falling on us, we would be alright. Baba looked at me strangely and remained silent.

We took a cab from the airport to Antonieh. The driver was Lebanese Muslim and hesitated to drive us back to East Beirut. He was afraid the Lebanese Christian militia might kill him for being a Muslim. The driver insisted on only taking us to the dividing line between East and West Beirut and no further. Baba and I had no choice but to agree. The driver shot out like an arrow, moving quickly since the roads had emptied except for the militiamen. As we approached a Palestinian bunker with men carrying machine guns, the driver showed them his identification, which indicated he was Muslim. His identification saved his and our lives. Once the Palestinian militiamen allowed us to drive on, our hero driver continued at the speed of light, dropping us two blocks from our home in Antonieh, just short of the dividing line between East and West Beirut. Before I left the driver, I thanked him for saving our lives. He said he did it because he hated the color of blood. He couldn't bear to watch them shoot us in front of him. I thanked him again.

Mama, my siblings, and our neighbors were waiting for our arrival. They were overjoyed to see Baba. That evening, we threw an extraordinary party where my sisters and some of their friends belly danced. Mama made a feast of tabouli, hummus, baba ghanoush, chicken, rice, fried pine nuts, and falafel. Despite the occasional rumble of artillery, we managed to have a wonderful celebration. A little bit of arak, Lebanese ouzo, didn't hurt, either. Before the party was about to end, Baba and some neighbors talked politics. They all agreed America and Israel were helping the Lebanese Christians secretly fight against the Palestinian militias. If it wasn't for America, Baba said the Palestinians would have killed all the Lebanese Christians and occupied the entire country. Hearing my Baba and the neighbors assured me I made the right decision to apply to go to college in the U.S. However, since it had been ten months since I applied, I concluded that my application was sent to the trash bin.

My Baba loved parties, drinking, and eating. When he stayed with us, he encouraged Mama to cook for and invite all the neighbors. He brought money from Saudi Arabia. Every time there was a cease-fire, Baba gave me money to go to the market for food and arak.

196

One Sunday, several days after Baba arrived, our house was filled with neighbors and friends for a big meal and drink on a cold December afternoon. The music blared, people danced, and some sang. Baba occupied himself with his arak bottle. I sat with him, chatted, and occasionally broke away to interact with young ladies. When the telephone rang, Mama was in the kitchen making more delicious Lebanese food. Her face changed color as she answered the phone.

Mama looked confused and upset. She ran to the radio, turned off the music, and hurried back to the phone. By now, everyone in the room had turned quiet. The apartment became as still as a Sunday prayer. Mama's face turned red, and she demanded, "Who is this?" She looked at my dad, saying a man was talking to her in a foreign language she couldn't understand. My father, who spoke a little English, reached out for the telephone. The person on the other end of the line said, "Congratulations, Sir, your application to go to the United States to study engineering has been accepted."

My dad paused, a shocked expression spread on his face. He said, "What do you mean I have been accepted to go to the United States to attend school? I have never requested such a thing like this. You must have the wrong telephone number."

"Is this Mr. Khouri?" the voice asked.

"Yes, it is," my Baba replied.

"Then I am not making any mistake, Mr. Khouri."

"Why would a man already a physician's assistant

197

and in his sixties want to go to America to learn engineering?" Baba asked.

"Is your first name, Nabil, Sir?" the man asked.

My dad paused again and sighed, staring at me intently. He replied, "Oh, Nabil, he is my son. Yes, indeed, he is interested in going to the United States. I am sorry for all the confusion, but Nabil is very interested in going to America to study engineering." My dad, who used to hate America in the past, decided for me to go there without even asking me. "What do we need to do next?"

When I heard Baba mention my name to the foreign man, I became nervous, not knowing what was happening. I had completely forgotten about the U.S. Embassy. The conversation went on for a while, and Baba took notes. After my Baba hung up the phone, he shook my hand and kissed me on the cheek. He explained to Mama and me what was going on. Baba and Mama were proud of me. They decided I was going. I was overwhelmed and expectant. I finally glimpsed the light at the end of the tunnel of hope to become an engineer one day.

Early the next morning, I went to the U.S. Embassy with Baba, who filled out all the legal papers and signed all the documents. I was still in shock. At the Embassy, I kept looking around for the blonde receptionist once again, but I didn't see her. When Baba finished, we bought a one-way plane ticket from Beirut to JFK airport in New York, then another ticket from New York to Gainesville, Florida. I had never even chosen Florida, but apparently, Baba had. I had been accepted to go to school for a Bachelor of Science degree in engineering at the University of Florida. Although I did not know English, I was excited to leave the hellish life in Lebanon behind. I was anxious about going to a country where I did not know anyone and not even the language. I was told, though, that the University of Florida had a program called English Language Institute (ELI) for international students. My main concern was leaving Mama behind in her fragile health, as her diabetes affected her vision.

It was Christmas Eve, 1978, when my family threw a big goodbye dinner party for me. Mama made various Lebanese dishes; hummus, baba ghanoush, tabouli, falafel, manakeesh, and kibbeh. The tapes of Fairuz, a Lebanese singer, were blasting while my sisters and their friends danced a mix of belly dancing and Lebanese dabke.

My flight to the U.S. left the following day. Some of my family and friends teased me about going to such a great and exotic country. They told me I would spend the rest of my life there. They told me an American woman would fall in love with me and keep me in her country for the rest of my years. My sister, Jehan, warned me about American women because she heard they were all ruthless and didn't care for Middle Eastern boys. She reminded me I had many women relatives who were single, and I should never think of marrying an American woman.

Mama studied my face for nearly the entire night. Now and then, my dad sat next to me and told me he was going back to Saudi Arabia in the first week of January. He would wire money as soon as he got there. He informed me he only had seventeen hundred U.S dollars, but I should never worry about money. Baba would provide me with all the money I needed. He told me that the only thing I should worry about was school. He assured me I would be able to learn the English language in a year and complete my engineering degree in four short years. Baba reminded me that I should open a checking account with a local bank as soon as I arrived in Gainesville. He wanted me to call him in Saudi Arabia to give him my new checking account number so he could wire me money. His idea made me worried. I wanted to see the money in my hands before I left Beirut. I had a feeling the seventeen hundred dollars he offered wouldn't be enough for me to live in Florida and pay my tuition for more than one quarter. I asked Baba how long it would take to wire money from the Middle East to the U.S. He told me it wouldn't take more than a day. Again, he promised me not to ever worry about money because he would take good care of me.

I was disturbed inside because when I was nine years old, and Baba held his first job in Saudi Arabia, the rest of our family practically starved in Mafraq. Baba hardly sent us anything, not even a package of bread.

My sister Sonia, the newlywed, came over for my farewell party. She said she had known I was a special boy since I was born. She was worried about me in such a vast country without any friends or family. She urged me to make friends with Arab students and not American ones and warned me not to fall in love with an American girl. Sonia cautioned that I shouldn't even talk to an American girl. She was afraid if I started to be friends with American girls, and they began to get to know me, one of them might marry me, and I would never come back. She said I had a charming personality that made women around me melt.

Her husband joined us and handed me a sign attached to a string as we talked. He told me to wear it around my neck once I arrived in New York. The sign said, "I can't speak English. My final destination is the University of Florida, Gainesville, Florida." My brother-in-law spoke English reasonably well. I thanked him for it, feeling relieved I would have some help getting to Gainesville.

During all the excitement of the party, my stomach felt like it was being ripped apart, but I refused to show my hurt to anyone. I remembered why I filled out the application; I only wanted to see the pretty clerk again. However, the reality of my situation sunk in as I watched the people around me saying goodbye. I thought, "My God, I'm going to America tomorrow." The country I had learned to detest before I learned to read as a young child was to be my new home. But I remembered the conversation between the Jordanian adults during the war between King Hussein's army and the Palestinian militias. The Palestinians would have overtaken Jordan if it weren't for America helping the Jordanian government. Since then, my attitude towards America changed, and Baba's recent conversation with the neighbors confirmed the U.S. was not as evil as I had been taught to believe when I was younger. I felt excited and hopeful at what I might find in America or what America might find in me. I reminded myself when I escaped to Syria, I returned to Lebanon as a failure. Then I went to Spain, and again I came back to Lebanon as a failure. I told myself that there was no way out and no return as a failure this time.

My Baba came back to sit with me. "Are you scared?" I lied, telling him I wasn't. Patting me on the back, Baba reiterated he would be in touch with me weekly and send me any financial help I needed to finish school. Part of me did not trust him, did not believe him. Again, images of my family, hungry and poor for those long months when Baba was in Saudi Arabia, and we were in Jordan, floated before me. The more Baba spoke about helping me with money, the more my stomach ached.

By midnight, our friends and neighbors started to leave. Each time I hugged one of them to say goodbye, I did not want to let go. I wanted to stay attached to that person, to any person. The more I repeated my goodbyes, the more I did not want to go to the U.S. Finally, everybody left except for Sonia and her husband, and I moved to sit next to Mama on the brown sofa in the living room. I put my arm around her and asked for her honest opinion about my trip. Mama wondered what I thought about my trip. I told her I wasn't in any condition to think at all. I begged for her opinion. She tapped her hand on my knee and said, "Son, if there were anyone in this room able to make it in the U.S., it would be you."

Her words took me aback. I asked her why me. She looked deeply into my eyes and said, "You are the most flexible and adaptable child of all my children."

I smiled at her and told her if I were genuinely flexible, I wouldn't have left Spain. Mama laughed, put her arm around me, and whispered in my ear, telling me the reason why I left Spain was to get this opportunity to go to America. She told me to have faith; she reminded me that everything happens for a reason. Her last statement astonished me when she said I shouldn't limit myself to making friends only with Arab people. She said, "All people come from one God, and therefore, we are all equal."

Sonia and her husband began yawning and rubbing their eyes, tired from the long day. But I was wound up. Part of me wanted to sleep so deeply that I would miss the flight in the morning, but the other wanted to stay awake all night, so I would be sure not to miss it.

Around one o'clock, Sonia and her husband approached me to say goodbye and wish me the best of luck. I hugged Sonia tightly, thanking her again for her earlier advice. I kept my smile on, trying not to cry in front of her. I wanted her to believe I wasn't scared, but she wasn't fooled. Her last words to me were, "You are braver than you can ever know. I am sure you will be making many friends in no time."

I hugged my brother-in-law and thanked him again for the sign. He told me, "Be brave; I know you are not scared; you can do it." I thanked him for believing in me.

Shortly after they left, my Baba and Mama went to bed. Jehan was the only person in the room with me. She took out a cigarette, but her hand shook as she tried to light it. I asked her why she was shaking; she wasn't the one going to the U.S. She laughed, saying no, but her baby brother was. She told me she worried that I did not know how to cook. She said she never saw me washing any clothes or ironing any shirts, and she knew how much I enjoyed being around people. She wasn't sure how all of these things would affect my lifestyle in the U.S. I assured her everything would be okay. I was overcome by her sweetness and selflessness for me when I was leaving her behind in this terrible civil war.

Jehan finally retired at about two-thirty. I was getting sleepy and decided to sleep on the same sofa where I sat. It seemed like minutes had passed when Mama woke me up to go to the airport. Sonia and her husband surprised me a few minutes later when they knocked at our door, offering to drive me. Before we left the family apartment, gunfire broke out, and bombs began to fall intermittently. My brother-in-law and Sonia did not hesitate. The car ride was life-threatening amid the sporadic shooting, but it distracted me from my apprehension. I traded one fear for another. Anything I was afraid of, my going to America was nothing compared to the fear I had experienced in Lebanon and Jordan.

Sonia and her husband dropped me by the terminal in a hurry. As soon as my luggage was out of the car, they disappeared in the blink of an eye. It was my third time riding in a plane, and I didn't know how long a trip it would be from Beirut to JFK. I wasn't sure if I wanted to know. We left Beirut at about six-thirty in the morning of Christmas Day, landing in Amman, Jordan, an hour later. From there, we took on more passengers and headed to Amsterdam. The flight to Amsterdam took about six or seven hours. I asked God to please not let me sleep in the streets of America or in any of its warehouses.

As we landed in Amsterdam, the ache in the pit of my stomach returned. This time it felt like a drum someone was pounding on. There was a two-hour layover in Amsterdam before we took off, again, for New York. I turned my head in every direction, hoping and praying to see a familiar face. I fooled myself into thinking maybe I would see somebody I knew. My thoughts took me back to Mafraq, only seven years earlier, when I recalled joining rallies, singing and shouting, "Death to America! Death to the Jews! Death to Israel!" Here I was on my way to face them.

I wasn't sure how I would handle not knowing a single soul. I thought to myself, what happened to the brave Nabil I knew? What happened to the boy who carried guns at age eleven, the boy who used to jump from moving trucks, the boy who jumped over burning tires? Is he dead now? I knew he was still alive inside me. I kept telling myself I was a lot stronger and braver than anyone I knew. I was born to become an engineer and to live everyday life. I determined I would never go back.

11

TORN BETWEEN TWO CULTURES

SEVENTEEN HOURS LATER, my plane began its descent into New York City. I gazed out the window at the tall buildings and lights shining from the city. It looked like a massive circuit board. The magnificent picture of the city through my little window intoxicated me.

As we approached the airport, the reality of my situation consumed me. It was around 7:00 PM on Christmas day of 1978 when we landed. I was one of the first passengers to unhook his belt and stand up as if I were in a hurry to meet someone waiting for me. I had another ticket to fly to Florida, but I wasn't sure what terminal I should go to. I wasn't even sure what airline I was flying on.

I left the plane and asked a young man, another passenger, where to collect my luggage. He told me to follow him as he was going to the same place. I wasn't sure what country the man was from, but he understood my broken Spanish and French. I trailed the young man, step by step until I got my suitcase. I hugged all my possessions tightly to me. I had my suitcase, a pillow, and a blanket with me. Mama thought I might need these last few items the first few nights if I slept in the airport or the street since I couldn't speak the language. She warned me the first week was going to be very hard. The size of the airport overcame me; it seemed nearly a hundred times larger than the Beirut airport. It wasn't quiet. I kept hearing announcements over the loudspeaker. I didn't care for the announcements; they confused me and interrupted my concentration. I especially hated the noise around me from people and vacuum cleaners. I was astounded to see small vehicles carrying passengers and luggage inside the airport. Their blaring horns alarmed me. I asked myself why cars would be driving inside the airport building. I saw young people lying on the floor wearing torn jeans and T-shirts, long hair, and bandanas around their heads. I stood with my mouth gaping wide open. Is this America with cars driving in the airport and people looking destitute?

As I walked through the airport, I made sure the money Baba gave me was stowed safely inside my jacket pocket. Mama had taped the pocket shut for me so no one would steal my money.

I finally made it to a quiet area with fewer people than the luggage section. I sat on an empty seat with my suitcase, blanket, and pillow on my lap. I decided to rest there for a while. It wasn't bad at all; it was a few steps higher than sleeping on Spain's streets. I fell asleep a few times. At around 9:00 AM, the day after Christmas, an employee saw me with the sign hanging around my neck. She approached and spoke to me in English, even as she looked at the sign, which indicated I couldn't speak English. I handed her my other plane ticket for my flight from JFK to Gainesville, Florida. The young woman walked with me, almost shoulder to shoulder, and took me to the terminal of Eastern Airlines, where I was supposed to take the plane the night before. The feeling of being overwhelmed invaded me. I ended up missing my flight. At least three employees from Eastern Airlines worked on my ticket to get me to Gainesville. One of them said I needed to fly to Orlando and from there on to Gainesville. The minute the gentleman said Orlando, I shouted at him in Arabic and French. He was in complete shock, having no idea what had upset me. I screeched at him in Arabic that there was no way in hell I would go back to Orlando; no way was I going to cross the ocean again.

The gentleman did not understand what I was saying, and he called a lady over who spoke French. She asked why I was so mad at her co-worker. I told her I was simply not going back to Ireland and then from Ireland to Gainesville. She said, "Sir, he never said Ireland; he said Orlando." The lady determined that we pronounced Ireland as "Irlanda," which sounded like Orlando to me in Lebanese. She laughed, and we all exchanged apologies. The man laughed, too, and showed me on a map where the city of Orlando, Florida, was located.

It was decided I would fly to Atlanta instead of Orlando. They told me I could easily get a plane to Gainesville from Atlanta. I felt better going to Atlanta, but I was still suspicious I would end up in Ireland. I was exhausted. I did not want to sleep at the airport, afraid someone might steal my money and suitcase.

I decided to sit down and watch the Americans pass by. The differences in their sizes, shapes, and coloring fascinated me. But I was disappointed with the size of the American women's chests. Unlike Middle-Eastern and Spanish women, their chests were very tiny.

It was the morning of December 26 when I took the plane from New York to Atlanta. I was amazed it took two hours. In Lebanon, you could cross the whole country in two hours of driving. Once we landed, I was relieved I only had one more take-off before I reached my final destination. The waiting in Atlanta was not bad compared to New York, and a couple of hours went by fast. Somehow, Eastern Airlines arranged with the flight attendants on my plane to help me in Atlanta get to the correct terminal for my flight to Gainesville. The way I was taken care of in Atlanta, I felt as if I were mentally challenged; however, I had no choice but to trust the airline staff.

I was starving when I arrived in Gainesville. My stomach was bothering me on the plane, so I refused each meal. While I waited in New York, although I was hungry, I had no way of finding a restaurant or ordering food. As I walked out of the Gainesville airport, a middle-aged African American cab driver approached me, asking me questions. I had no idea what he was saying. He grabbed the sign hanging around my neck, pointed his finger at the last sentence, and nodded, indicating that he could drive me to the University of Florida.

He helped me with my suitcase, and we drove to the university's admissions office. As the man parked his cab, he spoke to me in English again, but his attempt to communicate was fruitless. He stepped out of the car and took me with him to the office's main door. He tried to pull it open, but the office was locked due to the Christmas break. I looked at the man with eyes as sad as a puppy's. I gestured with one hand towards my stomach and the other towards my mouth, signaling I needed food. The cab driver sighed, shook his head, and shut his meter off. He drove me to a pizza place called Leonardo's, just outside the campus.

When we entered and sat, a young lady, the waitress, came over to ask what we wanted. The cab driver spoke to the lady. The waitress left to return with pictures of food. I pointed to photos of pizza. I had no idea what was on it, but I was hungry to eat anything. I spread out five fingers, and they thought I wanted five pizzas. I drew five slices on a napkin.

As I ate my pizza, the man drank his Coke, talking to another man in the restaurant. I was able to understand the word "international" being repeated. The driver and young lady stared at me in uncertainty when I picked up a knife from the table. I needed to tear inside my jacket to get the money Mama had put inside. The man and waitress studied me very strangely. I fished out some money and handed it to the driver because I trusted him the most. He paid the young lady and gave me back my change. We left the pizza place and drove to the International Student Center office.

The driver was happy to see the building. We were disappointed to find the door locked. Climbing back into the car, the man took me back to the restaurant. He spoke with the waitress and other customers again. I guessed he didn't know what to do with me. The Holiday Inn Hotel was only a half-block away from the pizza restaurant. I pointed my finger to the hotel, but the driver again started talking to the waitress. They must have agreed the hotel was not a good idea for me, probably because I couldn't speak the language.

Then the driver gestured for me to go with him to the cab. We drove to two separate buildings that were both locked. My arrival in America during Christmas break was a mistake. It was almost four o'clock in the afternoon, and I was still hanging out with this cab driver who had no idea what to do with me.

He finally drove me to a police station. As soon as I saw the sign, I became alarmed. I did not want to go to the police, especially the American police. I thought, "What if they knew I was with the ALF when I was a boy?" I expressed my feelings, telling him, "No, no policia." He managed to understand and respect my appeal. Turning around in the parking lot, we returned to the main road. We drove for about ten minutes until we arrived in a residential area. It was noticeable that the area was mainly a black neighborhood. Young African American men stood on a street corner, and some black children played outside a few of the houses.

We pulled up to an old house. The man opened his trunk and took out my suitcase, but I still had no idea where we were going or what was going to happen to me. He gestured for me to get out and follow him. An African American woman appeared with a gorgeous child standing beside her when he unlocked the door. The driver hugged the child, played with her a bit, and kissed her as we entered. He started talking to the woman a minute later, pointing at me while he spoke. For some reason, I felt completely comfortable with them. Though I was tired and confused from the day's events, I felt warm from the way the man and woman smiled at me, making me feel at home.

Feeling at ease, I sat on the small cozy living room floor and began playing with the child. The smell of fried chicken wafted from the kitchen, making the home even more comfortable. His wife spoke a little French, explaining she had taken French in high school. She gestured at her watch that in three hours we all had to go somewhere. She asked if I needed to take a nap. She directed me to the sofa. I fell asleep almost before I hit the cushions. It was around six-thirty when the man woke me up. I used their bathroom, the water feeling good after the long journey. The four of us left the house even though I had no idea where we were going.

We took a short drive until we came upon a wide-open area where many cars were parked. A huge, black tent rose above the land like a strange mountain. Rows of chairs lined the inside of the tent. We sat down together, and within a couple of minutes, almost every chair under the tent was filled. At seven o'clock, two men stood in front with a band behind them. I noticed Bibles being handed out to every individual and suddenly the music started. I couldn't understand why a concert would have Bibles. Once the music began, people stood, raising their hands above their heads, singing and shouting, and praising God.

I wondered what kind of church this was. Why was the church inside a tent? I felt awkward being the only white person among all these black people. I asked myself if all the churches in America were like this one. I could not believe that people were playing music, raising their hands above their heads, and swinging their bodies wildly while they prayed. It was an utterly bizarre experience for me.

The man and his wife introduced me to many people as the service ended. I did my best to introduce myself to them. There were swarms of them, each one with a foreign name. I could hardly remember more than two or three names. It was around ten o'clock when we finally returned to the house. This family was so kind and generous to offer the sofa for me to sleep on that night.

The following day the man took me to an apartment called The Place, located across the street from the university. Luckily, the management office was open, and I could move into an apartment with three other roommates. My three roommates were American, and, I would find out later, one was Jewish. I didn't feel very comfortable in the apartment, it was anything but home, and it certainly did not feel like family. The living room was big with an old sofa and two ancient oversized chairs. The dining room had a tapioca-colored table that seated four people. The four green chairs around the table looked like they were made in the 1800s. The kitchen looked dark and dirty. There were empty beer bottles on the counter and some trash on the floor. The four bedrooms were upstairs. Each room seemed the size of a closet. I was surprised the apartment had an air conditioning unit, as I had never seen this before. We always kept our windows open in Jordan and Lebanon, even when warm outside. And I was a little wary when my roommates said I needed to make sure the apartment's main door was always locked. This certainly was not a ritual where I came from. The three boys were very kind and friendly, but I distanced myself from them. I had decided not to get too close to any American.

Two days later, one of my roommates, David, started communicating with me using hand gestures and a couple of English words followed by some French words. He asked if I was interested in walking with him so that he could show me around. I liked the idea. We started walking away from the campus towards the town and residential areas. It struck me that individual houses had yards but no concrete walls which commonly surrounded homes in the Arab world. The front and back yards were completely open; any stranger could walk onto the property! What about the residents' privacy, which was so important in my part of the world? And trees and grass grew everywhere, unlike Mafraq where the landscape contained sand surrounded by the beige hues of residences and shops. As we continued walking and approached the town, I saw sidewalks as far as the eye could see. I hardly remembered one sidewalk in the town of Mafraq. As we turned a corner, I was surprised at all the traffic lights we passed. In Mafraq, there were none, and the few I saw in Beirut were usually not obeyed by drivers. It was new to see drivers stop at red lights and allow pedestrians to cross the street without fear of being run over. I started to think that a better God created Americans.

As we approached a shopping plaza, I became panicked when I heard the siren of an ambulance pass by. I thought Israeli warplanes were attacking us, and almost ran for cover. Walking along Thirteenth Street, we stopped at a massive store called Albertson's, a few blocks from the campus. I was impressed with the store, its size, and how alive it seemed inside. Everything from food to shoes to clothes to school supplies was there. I was used to small and cramped family-owned grocery shops that catered to a specific product like raw meat at a butchery or a vegetable and fruit store. Albertson's had frozen meats and vegetables inside endless freezers. It was hard to comprehend, as I had never eaten anything frozen before, except ice cream. I bought some food, and my roommate was kind enough to help me with the grocery bags as we walked back to the apartment.

David retired to his room, but I was hungry. I wanted to cook something, except I was afraid of using the stove since I wasn't too familiar with it. My other two roommates were not home, so I knocked at David's door, and somehow, he was able to answer my question about the stove using an Arabic-English dictionary I brought with me. Joining me in the kitchen, we cooked together, making steak and cheese.

The second morning David took me to the campus. In one of the buildings, students listened to music in a private room with headphones, and in another, students bowled. I certainly never saw anything like this at the Lebanese University. The last building we visited was the Reitz Union; students shot pool while others played ping pong. The minute I spied the ping pong tables, I became energized, as I was a championship player in high school. I had also frequented a ping pong club in Beirut during cease-fires and was considered one of the best players. David managed to understand my inter-est in ping pong and hooked me up with students who were playing. David studied me with proud eyes as I vigorously smacked the ball right and left and scored the most points. I felt I might just start fitting in with American college students as I left the building.

After a few hours on campus, we agreed to return to our apartment. The other two roommates were sitting in the living room watching TV, and David joined them. I could tell that David was bragging about my ping pong prowess.

The school opened a few days later, and David helped me register. He and I became friends. When I first found out David was Jewish, I was skittish about living in the same apartment; however, in time, his generosity and compassion made me view him as one of my first American friends. He supported me in learning English, and many nights we had dinner together at home. Even though both my sisters warned me not to become friendly with Americans, I decided to follow my mom's advice when she told me everyone was the same. I was beginning to think this even applied to Jewish people. However, I was ashamed to tell my family or friends back home that I had a Jewish roommate, as I thought they would think lesser of me.

In the first quarter, I took simple English classes designated for international students at the English Language Institute (ELI) and immensely enjoyed the challenge of learning English. I met many international students like me from various countries and made friends with some. It was comforting to know we were all facing the same experiences in a foreign country.

Going to my ELI classes gave me further opportunities to walk through the University campus. I was surprised to see young men and women wearing shorts and tank tops to their classes. I thought this was a sign of disrespect to their professors. When I went to the Lebanese University, most men wore collared shirts with long dress pants, and women typically wore dresses, skirts, or pants with a blouse. And the first time I saw a woman jogging through the campus in shorts, I thought she was mentally sick, as I had never seen this.

I was amazed when I learned that there were 40,000 students at the University of Florida. This was almost double the population of Mafraq. Because the University was so huge, I often had to run from one academic department building to another so that I wouldn't be late for classes. This was so different for me, as most of my classes were given in the same room at the Lebanese University.

When I finished class one afternoon, I was startled and disoriented when I saw students lying on the campus grass and making out. This would never happen in Mafraq, and if it ever did, there would be severe consequences. As I neared my apartment that day, I noticed a group of strangely dressed men with partly shaved heads and ponytails gathered at a corner of the campus lawn. They were chanting in a strange language and looked to me like they were from a different planet. I didn't know what to make of them. I wasn't sure if I needed to buy a ticket so I could sit and watch them or what. I learned later these were Hare Krishna followers.

I tried to spend most of my time away from the apartment, as my bedroom had a tiny window, but even with the curtain open and the light on, it was very dark. I put off going home as long as I could. When my classes ended for the day, I would either go directly to the library with some foreign students to work on my homework or find an empty classroom to study English and memorize vocabulary.

Although David had been friendly and supportive, as had my other roommates, we all became busier with our classes as the quarter progressed. Because we hardly saw each other for days at a time, I had moments of extreme homesickness. I became frustrated, as well, since I still couldn't speak the language fluently, which made me feel isolated. As the quarter wore on, I wondered if America was meant for me, and I considered returning home. One night when my roommates were away, loneliness gripped me, and I called my Baba in Saudi Arabia. I begged Baba to send me an airline ticket back to Beirut. My voice was small and weak so that Baba could hardly understand me. He scolded me to act like a man. I told him it was hard to talk to anyone, and it was hard for me to understand them when someone talked to me.

Baba asked how I was doing in school. I told him I was doing great in school, but that wasn't enough reason for me to stay away from my home and family. He reminded me the only reason I was in America was to go to school. He told me it was good I didn't have many friends so that I could devote my time to class. I argued back that I didn't even know how to operate the laundry machine. I told him I had been there several weeks without washing my clothes because I didn't know how. I was too shy and embarrassed to ask, as I had never seen a washing machine before.

"Please, Baba, can I come home because living on my own and taking care of myself is harder than expected."

He screamed at me to get a hold of myself and be a man. Baba said he had more confidence in me than anyone else. He told me if I ever came back to Lebanon without my degree, he would disown me. I instantly remembered those exact words echoing back in Mafraq when I was caught in the militia. His words tore me up. I didn't want to be disowned, but I didn't think I wanted to live in the U.S. There was a moment of scratchy silence. Baba asked me what I would do if I went back to Lebanon. He reminded me that Lebanon was a country without a government. He told me if I went back to Lebanon I would have no future. He said I was stupid to think of going back to that broken country. I had no choice but to agree. Dejectedly, I hung up.

I began seeing the wisdom in Baba's words in the next few days. I realized, over time, how lucky I was to be in America. It was incredible that there were street lights on almost every road in Gainesville. I couldn't believe I was in Florida for a few weeks and neither the water nor the power was ever cut off, unlike in Lebanon or Jordan, where this occurred regularly.

The first quarter at the ELI ended in March, and I

did very well in all my English classes. I couldn't believe I was able to mostly understand and speak the English language. The second quarter was a bit harder than the first. English grammar was confusing, as it had a lot of exceptions that drove me crazy. But with my hard work, studying late into the night, and the help of my roommates, I managed to do well.

The summer quarter was tranquil on campus, as many kids went home. I continued to learn English at the ELI, and I worked diligently as I was planning to take the TOEFL, Test of English as a Foreign Language, by the end of the summer. I had to pass this exam because I wouldn't be able to enroll in college to study engineering without passing it.

It was in August when I took the TOEFL exam and passed it. I felt exhilarated. In September, I enrolled in college to take my first quarter classes toward my degree. The journey towards my long-awaited dream was underway. The math and science classes were easy, unlike the English, humanities, and social science classes, where I had to work extra hard. Writing an essay for any English class was a pain in the neck. I had to write, rewrite, check grammar, and rewrite again until one of my roommates approved my essay before submitting it to the professor. Their kindness and support reminded me of the Arab culture back home.

When in my university classes, some of the rooms were so large I had to watch my professor on a large screen, as the lectern was too far away. It was not easy for students and professors to interact, unlike at the Lebanese University, where the classes were small, and the professor was always available before, during, or after class to answer questions. Although I encountered friendly and helpful students at UF, I found the academic environment more severe than in Lebanon. When at the Lebanese University, our classes would often be followed by students meeting for coffee and cigarettes. I determined the academic setting in the U.S. was more conducive to obtaining my degree and my personality since I was always serious-minded when it came to my schooling.

One element of American university life I would never get used to was how forward female students were when they asked male students for their phone numbers. Although I was flattered when this happened, I would never consider dating these women.

The first quarter in the engineering department ended with excellent results. Christmas of 1979 was about to arrive, and I had been in Florida for a year. However, I had only heard from Mama in Lebanon three times, one time by phone and the other two through letters. With the civil war in Lebanon ongoing, the telephone lines were often cut off, and it took more than a month for a letter to arrive from Lebanon. Baba, working in Saudi Arabia, was not a great communicator. He called me twice, and I called him once during the whole year, but he did keep his promise of sending money to my bank account every quarter to pay for my food, rent, and tuition. I had no way to work, as I was only permitted in the country through a student visa, and, therefore, working would have seen me in serious trouble with U.S. immigration.

During the Christmas holiday week, all my roommates went to their homes to be with their families. That freed the whole apartment for me. I decided to teach myself more recipes rather than make my standard meals of hot dogs, eggs, and hamburgers, typical American fare. I never had ketchup, mustard, or mayonnaise in my life; David introduced me to these condiments. I remembered how Mama used to make rice and chicken stew (*yakhni*). Even though the first time I made this dish, it didn't taste anything like Mama's, by the second time, the taste was closer. By the third attempt, I had a home run.

In February, 1980, the International Student Center, which was part of the University of Florida, threw a party for all the foreign students on campus. I asked David to go with me, but he said it would be better to go by myself, forcing me to make friends. He told me I might meet people from my own country. Although I was very nervous about going alone, I resolved to go anyway. I loved listening to the Spanish, Italian, and Russian music they played. I was there for two hours and they hadn't played one single song in Arabic. I craved Arabic music more than I craved speaking the language. I spent most of the night standing in a corner, watching people mingling. Sometimes I wove in between people, hoping to hear somebody who was speaking my language. I stayed another hour but didn't meet anyone who spoke Arabic.

I headed to the main door when I heard a young woman speaking to two other women in Arabic. I froze. I thought I was dreaming. I stood in place, trying to listen carefully to the women who were conversing. With a wide grin, I said, *"Marhaba,"* which means "Hello" in Arabic. All three quieted for a moment, and then said *"Marhaba"* back. I introduced myself, and they told me they were from the Arab Gulf. I was excited when I found they all lived in the same complex as I did.

Fadwa, the friendliest, had on a white dress that made her look very attractive next to her dark skin. She was also the most talkative of the girls and showed an interest in everything I spoke about. Sola, the loudest and most aggressive of the group, told me she had a fiancée back home and couldn't wait for the summer to see him and spend time with her family. She also had dark skin and wore a black dress. Her hair was ebony and straight, reaching down to the middle of her back. Lena was the most quiet of the three ladies. When she talked, her voice was just above a whisper. She wore black pants and a white blouse, and her skin was alabaster. Her skin color, brunette hair, and light green eyes made her look Western. I instantly felt comfortable with each girl, and we chatted for a couple of hours.

The girls invited me to another party they were going to. I was disconcerted, yet pleasantly surprised, that Sola had a car. This certainly wasn't the case where I came from. I had noticed that most university students had a vehicle they used for the smallest of errands, even those only a block away. The four of us got in Sola's car and took off. At the party, the three girls and I stayed together. The music was loud, hard rock and roll, which none of us cared for. We agreed the party was too wild and the students were drinking too heavily. Sola suggested going home. It was about eleven o'clock when we arrived at our complex. The girls asked me in to visit with them for a short while. Their place was spotless; its floor shined like a mirror. The furniture was in much better shape than my pieces. Pictures of Arab cities were nailed to almost all of the walls.

The four of us sat in their living room and turned on the TV, but we never glanced at it. Almost immediately, we became engaged in an intriguing conversation about politics and economics in the Middle East. My new friends felt sympathetic towards me over the bloody civil war in Lebanon. Although they were Muslim and, therefore, very conservative, they knew I was Christian, and they didn't seem to care. This was rare where I was from. A friendship involving the opposite sex and different religions nearly never happened.

I told them my Baba was in Saudi Arabia working while the rest of my family was still in Beirut. I revealed how homesick I was for my family, particularly my Mama who was my best friend. The girls listened attentively and assured me it was normal to feel that way for the first year before I got used to America. They had been in the U.S. for over two years and were lucky because they had come to America together after high school. I was amazed to find out they had known each other since childhood. The three girls were classmates their entire lives and their government gave them special scholarships to study together in America.

I said I wished I had a government like theirs. I disclosed I wasn't even sure if Lebanon had a government at all now. Fadwa asked me who was paying for my college and living expenses in Florida. I told them it was my Baba. Sola asked what I planned to study after I learned English. When I told them engineering, they were surprised. Fadwa said she would never have guessed that; she said I didn't have the personality of an engineering student. When I asked what she meant, she said I was too much of a "people person" to study engineering.

It was nearly three o'clock in the morning when we all agreed to call it an evening. My friends told me to knock at their door around noon if I wanted to visit more with them. I happily agreed and left. That Friday had been one of the best Fridays I had for a while. I was overjoyed to know these nice friends and thanked God for bringing these Arab ladies into my life.

I woke up just in time to get ready to visit my new friends by noon. When I arrived at their apartment, Fadwa, who was in her second year of an education degree, opened the door with a big smile on her face. I could hear Sola's voice from the kitchen asking me if I liked sugar in my coffee. Once inside, Sola told me she was studying for a test scheduled for the following week. She was in her second year, studying finance. Lena, who was in her second year studying international law, sat in the living room and looked at me intently. When Lena smiled, I felt happy. Sola's voice sang out, again, from the kitchen, saying she hoped I was hungry. I told her I was always hungry, and the three of them giggled. They asked me to sit around the dining table just outside their kitchen.

The four of us sipped coffee except for Lena, who drank tea. Lena sat across from me, her curious eyes making me feel uneasy. Sola told us during breakfast she needed to go to the library to do her calculus homework. Right away, I asked her if she needed help. She said she could always use help in math because she hated the subject. I made a deal with the girls that I would help them in math and science if they helped me in English. Lena asked me to tutor her when I finished with Sola. I had to concentrate before telling her it would be my pleasure. The way Lena looked at me, I had a difficult time looking back.

There was something about Lena I couldn't comprehend. The way she talked to me, and the Arabic phrases she used during her conversation, reminded me so much of my Mama and sisters. She sounded as if she grew up in the same village or house my sisters did.

One afternoon I went to visit the girls, and Lena was home alone making dinner for Fadwa and Sola. She asked me to stay, as the other two girls would be home momentarily. I felt a bit uncomfortable, but agreed to stay. A few minutes later, Sola and Fadwa came back from the campus and said they could smell the food from outside. They both said Lena was a great chef, and could cook just about any dish in this world. I told them how lucky they were to live with such a great cook. I noticed Lena wasn't just a wonderful cook, but she was fast and neat. She didn't leave any dirty dishes on the counter or in the sink. She cleaned everything around her while she cooked, exactly like Mama in the kitchen. I was impressed when I heard Lena knew how to make Lebanese food. I watched her cooking that night, and learned how to make healthy and more elaborate meals. After some time, Sola and Fadwa went down to the garage to pick up something from Sola's car. Lena and I were left alone in the kitchen. I was nervous being alone with Lena. I didn't want to say anything stupid.

After the two girls returned, we had great conversation and laughs and the night sped by. I went home overjoyed I had met these great friends. Stretching out in bed, my mind was filled with thoughts of the last few evenings. I thought about Lena. I began to think I might have some type of crush on her. Although she was shy and hardly talked, her eyes were filled with expression. I reminded myself not to fall for anyone in the U.S. because my main goal was to get a college education; besides Lena was Muslim and, therefore, it could never be. A Muslim woman would never be allowed to have a relationship with, or marry, a non-Muslim man. I ultimately came to think of Lena as a sister just like Fadwa and Sola.

12
MEETING MARY

IT WAS THE SECOND SUNDAY OF MAY, 1980, when Sola called and
asked if I wanted to go to the library with her and the
two girls. I told her I would be ready in no time. Since
Sola was the only one with a car, we piled into it and
headed off. I had no plans to buy a car since I didn't know
how to drive and had no money to buy anything besides
food. Baba sent me the minimum to cover the basics. I
was surprised and happy that Baba had kept his promise.

We drove to the Education building library to
study for hours on end many days of the week, sometimes together, and other times separately.

That evening, my friends informed me they would
be going home by the end of May to spend the summer
with their families. They had told me before, but I was
never prepared to accept the news. I said I was going to
miss them, but was happy they would spend time with
their families.

I returned to my apartment later that Sunday evening, and began studying for chemistry and logic exams that were coming up. It was midnight when I laid down in bed, thinking about my family in Lebanon, not knowing how they were doing, as it had been months since I last received a letter from them. I also reflected on how fortunate I was to be in the U.S. studying engineering, living in a safe environment - no snipers trying to shoot me, no crossing "the life and death line" to go to college as I did in Beirut. I was thankful Baba didn't listen when I asked him to send me an airline ticket to return to the war zone. I wondered how it might be to spend the rest of my life here in America and to live the "American dream." I concluded in order to live that dream, first I needed to become an engineer, a good one, and to make the U.S. my new home. This thought relaxed me and put me to sleep.

Before my Arab friends left the U.S. for the summer, Sola emphasized I needed to start making more friends on my own while they were gone. I told her I would do my best. However, as the three girls climbed into their cab for the airport, I felt myself sinking into loneliness. Calling someone was useless. Many times, over the past months, I tried to call home without any success. The phone lines in Lebanon were almost completely damaged due to the deadly war. Even though Saudi Arabia did not have a war within its borders, my dad didn't have a phone in his apartment. Whenever I called him at work, he got upset and told me not to ever call him unless it was an emergency. Baba wasn't keen on writing letters. I wrote him many times; however, he hardly ever responded to my correspondence. And many letters I sent to Lebanon were lost and never got to Mama.

I determined I must follow Sola's advice. I needed friends who would stay with me during the summertime, as well.

I thought of Samantha, one of my classmates in my social science and humanities classes. She was tall, solid, and laughed all the time. She had a big circle of friends I had never spoken with, as they weren't in any of my classes. On several occasions, her friends came and waited for her just outside our social science class to meet her after class ended. Many times, Samantha sat next to me and helped me with the social science class assignment. In return, I helped her with math classes. She wasn't taking calculus or advanced math classes like me, so explaining more basic math was a piece of cake. Samantha was majoring in history, and she received good grades in our social science class.

I had asked Samantha for her phone number, so I could call if I had a question about the social science class. The only issue was this particular class ended the previous quarter, so I didn't have any excuse to call her. Regardless, I decided to call her to say hello.

I was nervous on the phone, and wasn't sure what to talk about. In the past, our conversations focused on our social science class, or her math assignments. However, by now, it was summer quarter and I remembered she planned to take the summer off. I was thrilled when Samantha took over the conversation on the phone. She was the talkative one, and I was the listener. I managed to get the courage to ask her out that night. She told me she was planning to go to a disco with friends, and invited me to meet them there.

When I arrived at the disco I looked for Samantha, and caught her dancing with some of her cohorts. She was happy to see me and introduced me to her friends. Samantha and I danced for most of the night, and once I walked her to her car, she gave me a tight hug before getting in the car and told me to call her again soon.

One Sunday afternoon, Samantha called and invited me to her house to have dinner with her and her roommate. Samantha lived with Wendy, her roommate and friend. Wendy was very sociable and full of laughs just like Samantha. The three of us dug into the salads and spaghetti Samantha made. After dinner, the three of us watched TV until Wendy went to bed. To my surprise, after her roommate left, Samantha scooted next to me and began smothering me in passionate kisses. She asked if I wanted to spend the night with her. With heat rising in my face, I told her I needed to decline as I had a class in the morning, and had not taken the summer off as she had. I got on my bicycle and wobbled home thinking, "Wow, American women can be very aggressive." I was somewhat alarmed; this was so different from Arab society.

After my classes ended on Monday, I went to the

library and settled in a quiet corner to work on my calculus II assignment. As soon as I arrived back at my apartment, a roommate told me to call Samantha, as she had called earlier. The minute I called her back, she asked if she could come over to see me. That night Samantha and I had sex; it was my first experience ever having intercourse. The physical feeling was heavenly; however, I didn't have the same feelings of lust towards Samantha as I had had for Katia. I knew, though, that my lust for Katia was due to lonesomeness and largely being shut away from humanity in the warehouse. Also, I didn't feel completely comfortable with Samantha's loud voice and forwardness. I wondered if all American women were this bold. Was this why my sisters told me to stay away from them?

Around midnight, Samantha went back to her place. As I settled into bed, I thought about my family and wondered if Baba was alright, as I became short on money. In the morning I called the bank repeatedly, but still no money from Baba. I decided to call him late at night knowing it would be morning in Saudi Arabia. Baba was furious at me for calling. He reminded me to call him only during an emergency. I told him it was an emergency, as I had been short on cash for the last two weeks. I told him I was running low on food and didn't have enough money to buy more. Baba calmed me down, assuring me he would send money first thing in the morning. I hung up the phone only partly satisfied. I knew it would take longer than he promised. I thought at least in Jordan I went hungry with my family, and we knew people who either loaned us money or gave us food. Here, it was quite a different lifestyle, "survival of the fittest," where in Jordan and Lebanon everyone pitched in to help someone in need. It was hard to find people here to lend me money for the necessities of life. I realized I would have to get a job in Gainesville. I had no choice, even though Baba and I signed papers at the American Embassy in Beirut that I was ineligible to work in the U.S.; I would only have a student visa. Should I get caught working in America, immigration would deport me immediately.

I went back to bed but couldn't sleep. The next morning, I went to school feeling tired and sluggish from my long, worry-filled night. I decided to skip dinner for the next several days until I received money from Baba. The week ended and I still had not received a penny. The phone bill and electric bill had come and my roommates asked for my share. I didn't have anything to give them. Luckily, they understood and agreed to wait.

I determined I would ask if I could borrow money from them until I received funds from Saudi Arabia. They were generous and lent me twenty dollars each. Those sixty dollars helped me buy food for a week and a half until I received money from Baba. Even though Baba eventually sent what he'd promised, I was uncomfortable with totally relying on him. I was afraid of this even before I left Lebanon. In Beirut when Dad told me he would support me with money, my heart told me not to believe it. I was able to pay my tuition for the next quarter and repaid my roommates their money. I ended up with less than a hundred dollars, which was meant to sustain me for the next three months.

I picked up the phone, again. The minute Baba answered he screamed at me again, reminding me not to call him unless it was an emergency. I repeated what I said in my last call; living in hunger and poverty was an emergency. I reminded him he was supposed to send me more money than he had. I told him I needed enough money to cover rent, tuition, books, and still be able to survive. He didn't understand, suggesting I move out and rent somewhere else that was cheaper. I assured him that where I lived was one of the cheapest places in Gainesville. Baba refused to believe me, getting angry at me for telling him the truth. He ended the conversation by telling me I should have been gracious and satisfied with his help. He told me not to call him again.

As soon as I hung up the phone I tried to call Mama. As I expected, I could not get through to Lebanon. When I talked to my roommates about my situation, they suggested I go to the International Student Center and talk to someone who could help me.

The Director of the center was kind, but honest and blunt. He told me if I ever got caught working in the U.S. I would face problems with immigration. Nobody would stop them from deporting me. I felt as if I were caught in a miserable cycle. My only consolation was that my tuition for the following quarter was paid.

Samantha and I continued to see each other, but not on a regular basis, as I was becoming busier with calculus II, English composition, and chemistry classes. I told Samantha I was becoming low on funds. I explained I wasn't allowed to work in the U.S., as I was here on a student visa. She listened while examining my facial expressions. Later on that night, Samantha dropped me home, and she came in for a quick visit and some intimate moments.

After Samantha left, David was waiting for me in the living room. The first thing he asked was if I had thought about marrying Samantha to get a green card, which would allow me to get a job in the U.S. while I went to school. David's question shocked me. I instantly answered that she wasn't for me in the long term. I explained I would never marry a woman if I had any doubt about her.

The following Saturday, in early August, I decided to walk to a residential neighborhood and knock on doors. I was taking a big chance, searching for work in their yards. I was unlucky with those I approached, but did not give up. I went to the mathematics department in the same hallway where Sola had her calculus class. I posted an ad for tutoring math or physics on one of the bulletin boards. I was amazed when I received a call later that evening. The student asked me to meet with him in front of the library on Monday after my last class.

I tutored him two hours for twenty dollars. I asked if he would pass my name to other students who might need help. Soon after, I had more than five students, each of whom I tutored for an hour to two a week. I was still often short, but this extra money helped a lot. Once the quarter ended, I found myself back in trouble, since there were no students to tutor during the break from one quarter to the next. I decided, again, to knock on doors asking for work in people's yards. Like before, I had no success.

I went to Albertson's to see if I could find work. The first thing the manager asked me for was my visa and passport. I told him I would go home to get it. Of course, I never returned because I knew he would see my passport showing a student visa. I went back to my place, dejected. The only bright spot in all my trouble was knowing my Arab friends would return in one more week.

In August, in between the summer and fall quarters, I spent the weekend with Samantha and Wendy at their home. We had a great time together playing cards, watching TV, chatting, and sharing meals. Just before Wendy went to her bedroom to retire, she asked me if I thought of getting married to an American woman so that I could get my green card and work. I told her I did think about it; however, I wasn't ready to make such a commitment. Samantha jumped into the conversation and asked me if I wasn't sure about her, and I replied in a low voice I wasn't sure of anyone yet. Soon after, Samantha suggested she drop me home. While driving home, she told me she was willing to marry me as she felt very comfortable with me. Again, I explained that I wasn't ready to get married yet to anyone.

The following night, Samantha called me and asked if she could come over, but I explained it was the last week of the summer quarter, and I had a lot of studying to do with exams coming up. I told her I would see her on the weekend. The week ended quickly with all the homework I had to do.

The beginning of the weekend was interminable because David had graduated and moved to New York. My other two roommates had left for the break between the two quarters. Samantha moved into my place temporarily when she found out I was all alone. My Arab friends arrived a few days later. They were not impressed with Samantha, as she wasn't very neat; my apartment was messy with dishes in the sink.

A couple of days before the fall quarter started, Samantha gathered her belongings together in a small bag. She told me she was looking for a man willing to agree to a long-term commitment. She continued to say it was apparent I didn't share the same feelings she had for me. She wanted to stop seeing me since I refused to make this commitment. I felt sad when Samantha left, yet relieved since we were so different.

As soon as Samantha departed, I visited my Arab friends. I told them I had missed them very much, not only because they spoke my language, but because they were my true friends. They were like family to me; they were my sisters from another mother. I disclosed that Samantha had just broken up with me. They didn't seem to be surprised.

Fadwa and Lena told me they were engaged. Sola, of course, was already engaged. I said I was happy for them. I was a bit caught off guard, though, about Lena's engagement, but I knew this was the natural course of events and a turning point in my relationship with the three girls. Although we still saw each other, it was understood we would be hanging out together less, and concentrating on our studies.

The college reopened, and our classes were more challenging than the previous ones. Although I was very busy studying for my classes, I still had extra time to tutor students in math and science, even my Arab friends. Though I was worried about getting caught by immigration, this was the only way for me to survive.

My Baba sent me enough money to pay for the new winter quarter, but as usual, once I paid for the quarter fees, I had no money left for food or rent for the next three months. Tutoring alone was not providing enough money for me to live on. Since I excelled in math and science and regularly scored the highest marks, I widened my net and approached as many students as I could inside and outside my own classes, bragging about how good I was in class. I even told them I would charge half price. This worked as I started tutoring more students than expected. I became so popular that students approached me who were half a year ahead of me.

I moved out of my apartment during that quarter and relocated into a tiny efficiency apartment without any roommates. The rent for the new apartment was a bit cheaper. I kept myself busy studying, tutoring, and fixing up my new apartment.

In January 1981, my father called to tell me he had only one more year left in Saudi Arabia. He said he could support me until the end of the year, but I was on my own after that. I explained to him it would be impossible for me to make it independently. I said it was hard enough the way things were. I told him I was working and still barely making it. My Baba told me his contract would end, and he couldn't do anything about it. I had no say at all in my situation. He still sent me money to pay for the entire class load for that quarter, though.

I met several Arab male students in my math and physics classes. I became somewhat friendly with a few of them. We didn't have too much in common, as they weren't earnest students. These new acquaintances went out partying most nights while I spent my time huddled with my books in the library. They asked if I wanted to join them some time for a soccer game. I eagerly agreed, even though I hadn't played soccer since high school.

It was the third Sunday of March 1981, late morning, when I was home studying, and I heard a knock at my door. I opened it to find four of the Arabic male students I first met the previous month in my classes. They asked if I would like to play soccer with them. I smiled, telling them it would be more fun than studying, and I indeed needed a break. After I changed my clothes, we went to the soccer field. I felt as if I were back in high school again.

We began kicking and shooting the ball as hard as possible to impress each other when two women passed by the field. One of the girls wore a sweatsuit, and her brunette hair was tied in a ponytail. She was slender and light-skinned, and from the way she carried herself, she resembled an athlete. The other woman was Spanish-looking with a full figure, dark hair, and dark eyes. When the ball came to my foot, I stopped it, and my teammates shouted at me to keep kicking it. I ignored them to stare at the two women who had crossed away from the field. They passed by without knowing I existed; they never gave me a second glance.

An incredible feeling welled inside me as I watched the woman in the sweatsuit walk across the field. It was as if my soul was leaving my body. My friends continued yelling at me.

"Look there," I said.

"Where?" they asked.

"The woman with the gray sweatsuit..."

"What about her, man? Kick the ball, man."

"Wait, that woman, I know her."

"What do you mean you know her?"

"She is my princess," I told them. "I'm going to marry her someday."

"What did you have for breakfast today?" they asked.

"I am one hundred percent sure this is the woman I will marry one day."

I heard my teammates talking to each other. Nabil is going crazy, they said. I shouted at the two ladies, asking them if they would like to join us in our soccer game. They stopped, exchanged looks, and spoke to each other. My heart pounded. I desperately wanted them to come over, as I knew I needed to meet the woman in the gray sweatsuit.

A minute or so later, they shouted back at us that they would not be able to play. I was crushed. I shouted back, "Please come and join us! We are short on players." They ignored me and continued on their way.

When the ladies had passed out of earshot, my teammates made fun of me. "Hah hah hah, there goes your princess, your bride," they taunted. "Come on, Nabil, tell us what you had for breakfast."

I didn't care much for the words of these young men. However, I thought they might be right. But something else inside of me told me not to give up on that woman. I held the ball trapped under my right foot. Something possessed me, and I had no choice but to kick the ball as hard and straight as I could to land smack at that woman's feet. I shouted, "kick it back, kick it back." She ran toward us with the ball until she was closer and then gave a solid kick. I made sure I was the one to receive it with my feet. As soon as I had complete control of the ball, I kicked it back to that gorgeous girl. As she aimed the ball to return it, one of my teammates whispered, "Nabil, you got her. Nabil, she's yours."

My friend's words made me even more sure I was destined to be with this young brunette. As soon as she kicked the ball back to me again, I told her, "You are good, great, and play just like Pelé. You ought to come and join us."

She replied, "I'm sorry I can't. My friend does not want to play."

I said, "If you start to play with us, she'll join us in no time."

Sure enough, as soon as she approached my teammates and me, her friend came along to join us. I outstretched my hand and introduced myself as Nabil. The woman in the gray sweatsuit, who made my heart smile, was an American. Her name was Mary. Her roommate, who had a thick Brazilian accent, was named Barbara. Barbara was a lot more outgoing and friendly than Mary. However, my mind, my heart, and my soul were already consumed by Mary.

My friends started to tease me in Arabic. They said they would tell Mary what I said about her when she crossed the field. I was tempted to head them off and be honest with Mary. I didn't want her to think I was too forward, though. I kept my mouth shut unless I was made to defend myself.

As we began playing, I frequently kicked the ball to Mary and let her score when I was goalie. I pretended I was trying hard to defend the goal, and she was able to score. One of my friends said, "You bastard, how come you didn't play this gently with us earlier?"

I didn't respond. I was busy watching Mary's eyes become brighter, listening to her yell, and watching her raise her right arm in the air every time she scored.

Barbara started to feel bored and left out because nobody was kicking the ball at her. I was afraid she might leave the game, which would cause Mary to follow her. I started to play harder and make sure I passed the ball to Barbara now and then. Barbara responded by kicking the ball as hard as Mary had earlier. Soon she developed a cramp in her thigh that made her sit on the field, nearly in tears from the pain.

I ran to her, asking, "What is the matter?" When she told me, I started massaging her thigh. All my friends began to tease me in Arabic. "Oh boy, Nabil, you're going to score tonight." I shouted back in Arabic, "I am only helping her so she can walk and play again."

After five minutes of massaging Barbara's leg, she was able to stand up and walk again, but she refused to continue playing. Mary, the tomboy, was still shouting, yelling with each fierce kick or each time she scored. An hour later, Mary came over and told me she needed to go because she was tired and thirsty. The fun of the whole afternoon drained away. I asked her, begged her, to stay a little longer, but the beautiful tomboy insisted on going home.

Gathering all of my courage, I asked for her phone number. Mary was either ignoring me or didn't want to answer.

I asked Mary again, "Please, please let me have your phone number."

She smiled. "I have no time to socialize because I have so much to study."

I turned to Barbara, hoping for an entrée, and asked again for their phone number. Barbara's English was limited, so Mary explained, "He wants our phone number." Barbara thought Mary asked her what their phone number was. Barbara recited the phone number instantly. Although I didn't have a pencil or paper to write it down, I managed to memorize it. I noticed after Barbara gave me their number, she acted extremely friendly. She repeatedly told me how much she enjoyed the massage. I was only half listening.

I asked Mary, "Would you like to meet me at the student union tonight to play ping pong?" Barbara chimed in before Mary could respond, "Oh, yeah, I would love to." I was already wary of Barbara's burgeoning interest in me.

Mary said, "I'm not sure if we can meet you tonight at the student union, but you can call us this afternoon to check."

It was five o'clock in the afternoon when I tried to call Mary. I was nervous when Barbara answered the phone. She talked with me for almost half an hour about how much she enjoyed the soccer game, meeting my friends, and thanked me for easing her cramp. She said she had not played ping pong for a long time but was looking forward to it this evening. I was both surprised and confused by Barbara's intrepid approach.

When Mary came to the phone, her tone was very different from Barbara's. She was severe, and forthright. She, at first, declined but agreed to meet me at eight o'clock for ping pong. When I asked her if she could come by herself, she said, "No, Barbara is coming, too." As soon as Mary hung up, I called every male friend I had to convince them to join me at the student union to keep Barbara occupied. I was displeased when no one agreed to accompany me. Everyone seemed to have other plans.

By seven-thirty, I decided not to show up at the student union. I didn't want Barbara to misunderstand me; I did not want her to interfere between Mary and me. I felt terrible about my plan but I had no other choice. I stayed in my room feeling guilty, keeping myself busy with homework until ten o'clock. I picked up the phone and dialed her number and was surprised to hear the voice of an older woman with a European accent on the other end. I asked for Mary, and the woman said, "I don't appreciate people calling late at night! No one should call after 10 PM." I apologized to her and told her that my call was urgent. When Mary came to the phone, her voice was as cool as autumn. I could tell she was disappointed with me. I apologized to her, giving a weak excuse for not showing up. She kept quiet. She sighed, but I couldn't tell if it was out of boredom or irritation.

At the end of our one-way conversation, I asked her, "Can I see you tomorrow night, alone?" She said she couldn't make it. When I asked her why, if she had other plans, she said she had to study and wash her hair. I asked, "Can I call you the night after next?"

"You can try, but I'm not sure if I have time," she responded.

I said instantly, "I don't need any time from you. I don't need anything at all from you. All I want is to be your friend. And I want you to forgive me for my poor behavior for standing you up this evening."

I didn't want to tell her that I was afraid of Barbara. I was concerned if I told Mary, she would have thought I was vain.

Mary hung up the phone without giving me a chance to arrange another date with her. As bedtime approached, I tried very hard to avoid retiring as I knew I would be up the whole night thinking of this sweet woman who had turned my life upside down. I hated myself for not having enough courage to go to the student union, face both ladies, and tell Barbara I was only interested in Mary. I was upset at myself for massaging Barbara's thigh earlier that day, giving her the wrong impression. I continued studying for a few more hours after my phone call with Mary.

13
FROM RIDING A CAMEL TO DRIVING A CAR

I WAS GLAD WHEN THE NEXT DAY ENDED. I hurried home from school, ran to the phone, picked it up with shaking fingers, and redialed her number. The older woman answered. When I asked for Mary, she wondered if I was the guy from the previous night who had stood up Mary and her niece, Barbara. I apologized, telling her something out of my control came up, and there was no way I could keep my date. When I asked again if I could talk to Mary, she informed me Mary was still in school. Luckily, the older woman was kind enough to write down my phone number and said she would give Mary the message.

By seven o'clock, Mary still hadn't called. I had only three hours left to call her again. The strict landlady had made it clear she didn't like people calling late in the evening. By nine-thirty, my heart beat thunderously. I only wanted to hear Mary's voice on the phone. At nine forty-five I couldn't take it anymore, and I called her. The landlady, Ingrid, again, answered the phone. When I asked for Mary, she said, "Just a second." When Mary and I spoke on the phone, she told me she had to wash her hair. I told her I wasn't calling to ask her out. "I just want to hear your voice," I said. I asked about her day, and she complained it had been hectic. I asked if she was planning to wash her hair the next night.

"No, but I might be busy," she said.

"Can I try calling you anyway?"

There was a long pause on the other end. "Sure."

I called her the next day, early in the evening. Mary refused to go out, but she didn't mind talking to me on the phone for half an hour. Our conversation did not stray from topics relating to school or courses. I felt uncomfortable whenever she asked me to repeat myself when she had difficulty understanding my accent. But I loved talking to her; I loved listening to her. I even loved when she told me, "No," refusing to meet me. I asked if we could get together on campus the next day. She said she needed to focus on her schoolwork. She had no time for new friends in her life. I called the following night again anyway, my fifth time calling in less than a week. We spoke for only a few minutes before we hung up. It took seventeen phone calls before Mary finally agreed to go out with me to a restaurant called Sambo's for coffee and a study session. She made it clear we could only talk for twenty minutes, and after, we would have to study. I thought it was better than nothing at all.

We both agreed Mary would pick me up. She drove a 1974 golden Pinto. Climbing into the passenger seat, my knees hit the dashboard. She said I should move my seat backward, but I did not know how to reach the lever. Mary leaned across me, her arm accidentally brushing against my thigh as she reached for the lever to push back my seat. My mouth went to cotton and I felt embarrassed.

We headed towards the restaurant, and Mary was so focused on the road that she responded with either a simple nod or in brief staccato bursts of speech as I chattered.

When we arrived at the restaurant, I reached over the backseat to grab my backpack, and I was amazed at the stack of books and papers that Mary had brought with her. I thought she must be trying to take over the whole restaurant.

She saw me smiling and asked, "What's the matter?"

"It's nothing, just something silly," I told her. I didn't want to say I'd noticed the stack.

As soon as we were seated, Mary took off her watch. It reminded me of my grandfather's watch with its old brown band. I knew she planned to time us for twenty minutes of conversation before our studying time. When the waitress came to our table, I ordered coffee for both of us and asked Mary if she would like a piece of cake. Mary declined politely. "Coffee is all I would like."

Mary had dark hair, hazel eyes, and thick eyebrows which made her look as if she was Lebanese. She was thin, and whenever she smiled, her eyes would brighten like candles. Even though she looked serious, I sensed she was good hearted. We talked about our immediate families, and I listened carefully to everything she said. I found out Mary was originally from California, but her family moved to Georgia when she was twelve years old. I drew a map for Mary, and showed her how Lebanon bordered Israel from the south, the Mediterranean from the west, and Syria from the north and east.

Mary said she was working on her graduate degree in economics. She had an assistantship from the University of Florida and was dedicated and hardworking about reaching her goals. She emphasized that her schoolwork was the most important thing to her. I told her I was in my second year of civil engineering. I added I was also a serious student and often worked on assignments or studied for exams until after midnight. As we continued talking and sipping our coffee, Mary glanced at her watch every couple of minutes so as not to exceed twenty minutes. Even so, she acted very interested in everything I told her. During my conversation telling Mary more about my background, she pointed her index finger to the watch. She said time was up, and now we needed to study. She picked up all of her stack, left the booth, and sat in the adjacent booth with her back turned to me. I wasn't sure if I had inadvertently said or done something to offend her.

I stared in shock at the back of her lovely head. A few minutes later, the waitress came by, asking if everything was alright. I told her it was. Leaning down, she conspiratorially asked me if I was breaking up with Mary. I told her it was our first date. The waitress asked, "Why did she leave you to sit in another booth?" I told her I was telling Mary about myself when she decided to leave the booth. The waitress asked if I were a Russian or a Communist. I shook my head. The waitress left, and I was still puzzled. I couldn't understand why Mary moved to the next booth.

About a half-hour later, Mary turned toward me and said, "It is getting too noisy here; I think I need to go home." I told her that I would meet her outside as soon as I paid the bill. A few minutes later, I met Mary out in her car. On the way back to my place, I tried to be charming and acted silly to make her smile. I told her she was too serious and too structured, but inside, these characteristics made me more drawn to her. I told her I was nothing like her. I said I was a spontaneous person, and I could use some structure in my life. She didn't respond but continued to stare at the road ahead of us. When we arrived at my apartment, I invited her in for a short while. She said she needed to get home and study. As soon as I closed the car door, she sped away.

I went to my room, confused and disappointed. I wasn't sure what to make of Mary's odd behavior. Part of me wanted to call her and ask if I had done or said anything to make her move away from the booth. Although I felt disconcerted, the memory of Mary's face and voice seemed burned into my heart.

I decided to visit with my three Arab friends. The three girls complained about how hard their classes had become. They hardly saw each other. We were happy with our quarter grades, and agreed that each successive quarter would only get more challenging. I mentioned I had met a young lady named Mary who I liked a lot but felt she didn't like me.

It was almost ten o'clock when I arrived back at my apartment. I was tired from a long day of studying but reminded myself that obtaining an engineering degree was my primary focus and dream. That thought always put me back on track. After studying for a couple of hours, I stretched out on my bed, and my mind turned to my family, especially Baba, who I was almost certain would soon cut my financial rope. However, it was the thought of Mama that drew the strongest pangs of homesickness in my heart. I picked up the phone and dialed Lebanon, and I was both surprised and excited to get through for the first time in months. She, too, was thrilled to hear from me. I told her Baba might not be able to assist me financially after the end of the year. Mama felt sad. She told me whatever happened, I should not try to return to Lebanon. She said Lebanon was getting worse and worse by the minute. The fighting and killing were continuing at a feverish pace.

I hung up the phone, thinking, what options did I have now? If Baba wouldn't send money for school, and I couldn't go back home to Lebanon, where would I go?

After school ended the next day, I raced home to

call Mary. I resolved to confront her about her strange behavior. Mary acted as if nothing was wrong. She enjoyed meeting me and hearing about my family. She thanked me for explaining the history of Lebanon and the Middle East. I was surprised to hear that Mary had a good time. I was under the impression she was bored to death.

I asked her, "Since you had such a nice time would you like to go for ice cream sometime?"

"When?" Mary asked.

"Tonight," I told her.

"I'm busy studying tonight."

Somehow I managed to convince her to take a short break. My heart began pounding so fast that I thought I might faint.

Mary picked me up less than a half-hour later, and we drove to Howard Johnson's. This time I made sure that neither Mary nor I brought study materials; I wanted to ensure she wouldn't leave my booth again. We sat and ate ice cream for a couple of hours. Although Mary was quiet for most of the time, I loved every silent minute I spent with her. Her sweet smile and bright eyes were the primary form of conversation. When she drove me back to my apartment, I invited her in for a cup of tea. She refused and told me she had to study. I reluctantly let her go, missing her before leaving the car. I wanted to hug her and hold her tightly to me but was afraid of how she might react.

I spent the following day on campus. I had a lab

report to do for my engineering materials class that would take some hours. Even though I had a busy day at school, I was in an excellent mood after the perfect ice cream date I had with Mary. When I reached my apartment, I called Mary and asked if she had eaten dinner yet. She said she had just arrived home. I said I was making a Lebanese dish and asked if she would like to come over to eat with me. To my surprise, Mary was enthusiastic about the idea and told me she would be over in a half-hour.

I hadn't been cooking anything, so the minute I hung up the phone, I started cooking chicken with rice and tomato paste. I moved so quickly that I could have burned down my little kitchen. By the time the young lady showed up, I was halfway done with cooking. To keep her busy and distracted from how long it took, I showed her pictures of my family and Lebanon. Mary was amazed by the pictures, especially those taken at a party where my sisters and their friends were belly dancing. Mary asked about my parents, especially Mama. She seemed uncomfortable when she caught me trying to hide the tears in my eyes. I told her Mama was my best friend and I missed her very much.

As I went to check on the food, Mary followed me. I noticed her face was turned away. Mary had tears in her eyes. It was clear she didn't want me to see her tears. She felt terrible when I told her how much I missed home. Mary wiped her tears with the back of her hand and asked if the food was ready.

I proudly served her. Mary said the food was excellent. Living on my own for some time had turned me into a chef. When Mary finished eating, she said she needed to go home. She was swamped with work. I reminded her it was Friday, nearly the weekend. She said it didn't matter to her. She studied every day and night of the week. I told her even God rested on Sunday. Why couldn't she rest for a couple of hours on Friday night? She indicated she had just taken a nice break with me; she loved the dinner and enjoyed my family photos. She needed to get home to study. I reluctantly said, "Okay."

The following day, Saturday, I went to my three friends. We agreed they should meet Mary. Sola told me she noticed that I looked more content ever since I began seeing Mary. Fadwa said Mary must be different than Samantha. I said, "Much different. Mary is neat, and she's hardworking and serious-minded. And she's not pushy at all."

It was early May, about six weeks since I met Mary, when Fadwa, Sola, Lena, Mary, and I went out to dinner. I was delighted at how well the four of them got along. I remember Sola telling Mary she felt like she had known her all her life. Fadwa also said she felt connected to Mary the minute she met her. I was pleased when Lena told Mary that Nabil was very lucky to have her as a friend. After dinner, we all went to my friends' place, and the Arab girls taught Mary belly dancing.

For the following two weeks, I was buried in school homework, studying for my engineering material class, and completing engineering geology lab reports. In addition, I had an essay to write for English literature. Even though I didn't see Mary for those two weeks, my school work kept me occupied, and I hardly thought about anything else but my classes.

On the first Friday of June 1981, Sola, Fadwa, and Lena left for their country for the summer break. I took only two classes during the summer quarter: thermodynamics and engineering statistics. Summer quarters were the only quarters an international student didn't have to take a full class load. A full-time student schedule translated to at least twelve credits per quarter, four or five classes. Taking only six credits, two classes, in the summer was a breeze.

One Friday, I called Mary and asked if she was interested in going to Cedar Key, an artist's colony on the Gulf an hour away from Gainesville, the next day for lunch. We had only been together for a couple of months, and I thought we were getting along, so I was happy when she said she was interested. After fifteen minutes of driving, Mary stopped the car on the right shoulder, and I looked at her with surprise.

"Why did we stop?"

She told me she was not feeling well; she had a scratchy throat. Mary said she would have to return home unless I drove. I did not want to cancel the trip and go home to be alone again. I had no choice but to say, "Yes, I will drive your car."

Mary switched seats with me, not realizing the only

things I had ever driven had been camels, horses, and donkeys. I gripped the steering wheel tightly and told Mary I hadn't driven for a while. I asked her to refresh my memory. She said there was a first, second, third, fourth, and reverse gear. I put my right hand on the stick shift to practice the gears, and Mary shouted, "You better push the clutch in while you're doing this!"

I asked her, "Which one is the clutch?"

She said, "The one on the far left. Are you okay?"

I told her, "I'm sorry, I haven't done this in a while." I pushed the clutch and put the car in first gear, and Mary asked me to put the hand brake down, which she helped me with. The car started to lurch back and forth like a bucking bronco. I never expected this '74 Pinto would take so much effort to tame. As the car began moving forward, I managed, again with Mary's help, to change the gear into second, third, and fourth. The Pinto swerved right and left, and I was going about 10 to 20 miles below the speed limit. Mary kept telling me I was the strangest driver she had ever seen. It felt like it took forever before we finally made it to Cedar Key.

We had a fantastic lunch and visited the quaint Cedar Key. When it was time to go back, I asked Mary if she wanted to drive. She admitted she disliked driving and would prefer if I drove. Driving back was not as challenging as our drive from Gainesville to Cedar Key, as I learned how to press and release the clutch just the right way. As soon as we got to my place, I admitted to Mary it had been my first time driving any car. She wasn't happy I was driving without a license or experience and that I had put our lives in danger. Although I felt ashamed, I asked Mary if she would like to come inside, as I could make her a Lebanese tea for her cold. She agreed. I brought the tea to Mary, sitting on the oversized chair that took up a large part of the room in my efficiency apartment. As I leaned over, our eyes met, my left hand found her right hand, and I started to massage it. She looked at my hands while they were busy massaging hers. My lips reached out, and I planted a small gentle kiss on her head. She lifted her head upwards, and her eyes went through my soul. I took her face between my palms and kissed her softly on her lips. Her face turned to the color of red roses. I reached her lips again, and my kiss was a little deeper this time. Mary never drank her tea that night.

Mary and I began seeing each other almost daily. We studied for hours together during the summer quarter, and I cooked for her nearly every day. That summer, my relationship with Mary intensified and became complicated. Baba had not sent me tuition money so I could no longer go to school. The only money I had was what I made from tutoring, which was not much.

Two weeks later, I called Baba and told him I needed money by August for fall tuition. My dad shocked me when he said, "You should not expect a single penny from me anymore. You are totally on your own as of now." As soon as I hung up the phone, it was as if a great big balloon was suddenly punctured. I thought I was about to kiss my dream goodbye. I told myself maybe I was never meant to be an engineer. I struggled over sharing this information with Mary. I was afraid that the U.S. immigration offices might find out I was not enrolled in school for the fall quarter. I decided to keep my fear to myself and not tell Mary.

14
MEETING MARY'S FAMILY

IN JULY, MARY TOLD ME she was going to Daytona Beach for a week to meet her family for a vacation. Mary invited me to meet her in Daytona for the day so she could introduce me to her family. A friend of mine, whom I tutored in chemistry and math, agreed to drive me to Daytona Beach and back home. My friend was extremely understanding, staying on her own in Daytona while I met with Mary and her family.

Mary found me in the hotel's lobby where she and her family were staying. She was excited to see me. It was the first time Mary told me she missed me. She hugged me tightly, and I whispered in her ear if she was sure that none of her family had seen us embracing. Her response was to tighten her hold on me. Rivulets of sweat pooled underneath my clothes as she walked me towards the elevator.

The first person I met was Mary's mother, Mollie, who had short, dark hair precisely like my Mama. Her eyes were not that different from my mother's eyes. With great reservation, she shook my hand, hardly smiled, and in a polite voice, she said, "Finally, I meet you. I've heard a lot about you." The second person I met was Mary's father, Mark. He had a loud, high voice and was tall with a solid build. He shook my hand firmly and started lecturing me like the professor he was, about America and its government. Mary's younger brothers, Tom and John, both tall and slim, shook hands with me warmly. Her brothers shared Mary's dark good looks. Abigail, Mary's sister, looked similar to what I thought a typical American young adult would look like. She had blonde hair and blue eyes and shook hands with me the same way her dad did like she wanted to wait and see. I felt comfortable with Mark instantly when he announced he was pro-Arab and didn't care much for Israel. He continued to orate about the lifestyle of the U.S, and about the differences between America and the Middle East.

He abruptly asked, "Have you adapted to the lifestyle of the U.S.? I'm sure you haven't been able to yet, and that you might not ever be able to completely. I must tell you, I admire every foreigner who leaves their native country to go and live somewhere else."

Mary's mother studied me with eyes that seemed to pierce my soul as Mark spoke. Although she hardly said a word, her eyes indicated she was uneasy. I started feeling awkward in this hotel room with Mary's family and wanted to leave even though I knew that would have been inappropriate. Mary's dad was using very proper

English, so most of his words were lost on me. I found it easier to nod and agree with everything he said. I glanced at Mary a few times when her father scolded her brothers for various infractions. I wanted Mary to come up with an excuse to let us leave and spend time alone. The more I observed Mary, the more I realized that Mary seemed apprehensive about the situation. After all, this was the first time I was meeting her family.

A couple of minutes later, Mark stopped lecturing me. I corralled my courage and outstretched my hand; I said it was a pleasure to meet him. Mary seemed relieved as we walked out the door.

Mary suggested we go for a short drive. We found an isolated area by the side of the road. We sat on the hood of her Pinto. Mary told me her dad had given her the "thumbs up" sign, indicating he liked me before we left the hotel room, which made her happy. She asked me what I thought of her family. I told her I didn't understand much of her dad's terminology. I added I enjoyed and appreciated her father's perspective on the Middle East and her mother was so quiet. Mary said it takes time to know people.

Taking a deep breath, Mary said let's change the subject. She wanted to talk about us. I seized the opportunity and told her my Baba would no longer support me financially, and I had no way of paying my tuition for the next quarter. Mary's face became sad when I told her I might get in trouble with immigration if I didn't enroll in school for the fall quarter. She asked me the cost of my tuition. When I told her, she said she had no way of helping me either. She suggested I take only a couple of classes and work somewhere part-time. I explained the strict rules about foreign students, stipulating they be enrolled full time and not work. Mary asked what I planned to do. I told her I didn't want to go back home. I told her Lebanon was hell, and if I went back, I would have no choice but to join some militia, which might mean death. She told me I was crazy to think of going back. She asked me how immigration would find out if I didn't go to school. I told her they knew everything about me from my school records. It would be easier for me to move to a big city like Chicago or New York. I explained that immigration wouldn't be able to find me in big cities. She asked who would hire me without a green card. I paced and shook my head helplessly.

It was about noontime when Mary asked if I was ready to see her family for lunch. I told her I preferred to spend time with her alone. This made her smile. She asked if I planned to meet up with them for dinner. I explained that my friend agreed to meet me in the hotel lobby by five in the evening to head back to Gainesville. She said she would miss me after I left and more the following week when she was in Georgia at her family home. I promised her I would call every day she was gone. Her face seemed to light up.

Mary persisted that we should go back to the hotel and have lunch. We went back to the hotel room, but nobody was there; they had already gone for lunch. We decided to have lunch by ourselves. As we ate, Mary said she didn't want me to go to Chicago or New York to escape from immigration. She revealed she disliked big cities. Mary said she wanted me with her in Gainesville and that ever since we met, she had become a complete person. She told me she was happier and more confident in herself; nobody treated her the way I did. Her life had been measured out and calculated so methodically that she didn't know there was another way to live. When I came into her life, I showed her how to have fun, taste adventure, and be spontaneous.

Her voice shook with emotion, but she held herself together to make her point. The degree of intensity and emotion from Mary surprised me. I wondered what had happened to my logical, straightforward, blunt woman, whose heart I once thought was made out of rock and steel? Her heart seemed much more like mine. I realized Mary was trying to show me she was falling in love with me.

The waitress interrupted my thoughts when she brought our food. I hated eating out with Mary because she ended up paying for both of us most of the time. She knew how broke I was. As we began eating, Mary asked me, "How do the other Lebanese students survive in the U.S. without money?"

I told her, "These students are mainly supported by family members who work outside Lebanon, mainly in the Arabic Gulf and Saudi Arabia."

Around five o'clock, I told Mary I had to meet my

friend in the hotel where Mary's parents were staying. My friend was already waiting for me as we entered the lobby. I crushed Mary against me so that she was practically gasping for air. I wanted to hold her forever because I knew I wouldn't see her for the next several days, as she would be going to Georgia directly from Daytona Beach. As we embraced, Mary's father, who was also in the lobby, called to her, asking if she were ready to go to dinner. It was like an electric shock when I heard his voice, and I instantly let go of Mary. My feet moved backward towards my friend. Before I left the lobby, I turned to look at Mary and her father. We all waved to each other and I headed for the car where my friend was waiting.

The minute we were in the car, my friend wanted to know all the details of our meeting. I told her that I was nervous with Mary's family and sensed they felt the same about me. My friend held my hand comfortingly. She said, "It's our American tradition. Welcome to our country."

A few minutes after my friend dropped me home, I heard a cat meowing outside my kitchen window. He looked young and hungry, and I didn't remember seeing him before. I decided to leave the apartment to talk to the cat, but he began to walk away from me as I got nearer. I followed him to the apartment a few doors down from mine. I sat next to him and started petting him. He purred happily, and I held him to me. I was reminded of another furry friend I had loved so long ago.

I concentrated on the rhythm of his breathing, which made me remember all the changes I had in my life. I told the young cat that when I was a little boy, I was so desperate for love and to be hugged by someone I ended up falling in love with a monkey. My parents told me not to get too close to my monkey. I ended up getting close to a married woman just to be hugged and loved, but her mother-in-law kicked me out of the country. Last year, I developed some feelings for Lena, but our religions forbade us to move forward, so we ended up loving each other like a brother and sister. And here I was now drowned up to my ears in love with Mary, who I believed was my soul mate. She was not a pet, not a married woman, not a Muslim.

Mary was the perfect and genuine love for me.

I explained to the cat that many things attracted me to Mary—her gorgeous eyes and smile, to start with. She was serious-minded, academic, a planner, and not a party person. I appreciated she was money conscious, loving but logical, and open-minded about my culture. She loved my food and was open to my Arabic music and dance. She was strong in her beliefs and so precious in everything she did. The cat listened politely without any comment.

Soon after my chat, a man called the cat's name. The cat ran to him. I walked back to my place. I realized it might be another summer in America during which I would be lonely, but I thought it would be my last. For the first time in my life, I thought about having my own family. I wanted a woman and children. I wanted a life with people around me. I wanted a cat, a dog, a house, a future. I wanted all of this with Mary by my side. Then I told myself none of this would happen before I became an engineer.

I was so thrilled when Mary called a few days later to tell me she had just arrived in town. She was hungry and craving a Lebanese dish. I invited her over to have dinner. I loved preparing meals for Mary, and she was so appreciative, as she, admittedly, was not very proficient in the kitchen. Her focus was always more analytical; Mary wasn't the typical domestic woman. I made tabouli and baba ghanoush in around an hour when Mary showed up at my door. I hugged her so tight she could barely breathe. I kissed her head and bit gently on her hair like a puppy. Mary kept laughing as I tickled her face and skull with my kisses. She hugged me back as hard as I hugged her.

Once we sat to eat, Mary ate so fast, as if she hadn't eaten for days. It seemed she was enjoying my Lebanese food and had missed it. Soon after we finished eating, I asked her how she felt about moving in with me. Mary was surprised and didn't answer. I asked her again, and she said she just didn't feel comfortable with the idea. She told me my efficiency apartment was too small for two people. I told her I could make it work. I complained to Mary about my financial stress during the summer since not many students were around to be tutored. I told her I was getting tired of being broke all the time.

I explained that we could save a lot of money if we paid one rent instead of two. Mary said her family, who she was very close to, wouldn't appreciate it if we moved in together, and she just wasn't sure about taking this significant step. I reminded Mary that her life belonged to her and not her parents. Mary needed to think about all that.

Although we enjoyed our time together outside our classes, we knew that schooling was our priority. Mary had an assistantship that helped pay her rent and required her to teach a weekly review class in macroeconomics in an auditorium filled with undergraduates. One of her Economics professors at UF also asked her to contribute a section on utility pricing studies for his book on designing utility rates. Mary's extra work at the university and my advanced undergraduate engineering classes made us both burn the midnight oil.

The following morning, after our Lebanese meal, Ingrid, Mary's landlady phoned me. I was surprised to hear her voice. She was usually quite reserved, but Ingrid seemed extra friendly on the phone this time. She told me Mary had talked a lot to her about me, and she invited me over to have dinner with them the following night. I gladly accepted the invitation. Ingrid was from Denmark, and she knew a lot about the Middle East. She and I got along from the first "Hello." She was fascinated by me as much as I was by her.

That night, Ingrid learned a lot more about my family and me. I felt very close to her as if I had known her all my life. Just before I left, Ingrid asked if I would be interested in doing some work in her yard, offering me two dollars an hour. I was at her house the first thing next morning and worked for her the whole day. I worked for Ingrid for several weeks, cutting grass, trimming bushes, cleaning the yard, raking leaves, and organizing the garage. She and I developed an exceptional relationship. Ingrid bought me a pair of overalls for working in the yard. She also bought me the ingredients to make Lebanese dishes. She and Mary would sit at the kitchen table watching me prepare their requested meal. When the work in her yard slowed down, Ingrid went to every house in her community, helping me find more work. With a letter of recommendation from Ingrid coupled with my low wage rates, I suddenly had many customers.

I made enough money to pay for the next quarter's tuition, from cutting trees and lawns to planting flowers and basic landscaping. When the fall quarter began, my classes required more time and effort. They were nothing like my physics and math classes, which barely required any effort. Suddenly, I had no spare time for yardwork or tutoring. I became very short on money; I couldn't even pay my monthly rent. Buying a McDonald's meal was a challenge for me. I wasn't approved to open a credit line with only a modest checking account balance.

I felt embarrassed but decided with great reservation to ask Mary if I could borrow money for rent. Mary was sympathetic but said she was financially strapped since she was already paying for my groceries and her basic expenses. Unlike America, in the Arab world, you barely have to ask for any type of help, including finan-cial, before the whole community jumps in to assist.

Ingrid invited me for dinner again. Mary and Ingrid had drawn up a document stating I was about to borrow money from Mary for rent, as Mary had deter-mined to help me even though it meant going into a bit of debt. We discussed my rent issues, specifically that I still had two months to go before the end of the quarter, and Mary agreed to help with that. Ingrid also supported my idea that Mary and I live together to save money. When Mary hesitated, Ingrid told her, "I have lived long enough to tell who is good and who is bad, and I'm tell-ing you now that this young man is smart, decent, and hard-working but broke. Mary, this young man could be something if you give him a chance." Mary gulped. She said, "I'm going to have to think about living together."

Mary added, "There is something else, Ingrid, you need to know, and this regards the longer term. Nabil is a very kind person, I agree. He is caring, filled with emotion, and never shy to show his feelings toward me. But these are things that won't provide us with living necessities."

Ingrid interrupted Mary. "Mary, you're too young to understand what Nabil is going through. I grew up in Europe during the Second World War, and I know what war can do to people; I know how it feels to go to bed hungry, just like Nabil did in Jordan and Lebanon. Believe me, Mary, this young man will do well if you help him now."

Mary swallowed hard and told Ingrid, "My university assistantship couldn't support Nabil and me long term. I do care about Nabil, and sometimes I feel as if he is part of me . . ."

I jumped in and said I wouldn't feel comfortable making Mary do something she was not satisfied with. None of the ladies seemed to hear me.

I responded to Mary's concerns by saying once I finished the quarter, I might have to leave Gainesville anyway. I promised I would pay her every penny that I borrowed.

Mary's voice trembled when she asked me in front of Ingrid if I was still considering moving to a bigger city. I told her I would either do that or go back home. Mary asked, "How often have I told you I don't like big cities? You would be crazy to go back home with the deadly war raging in your country." I had told Mary a couple of weeks ago that the last time I talked to Mama, I learned our kitchen in Beirut had been hit by rocket fire, leaving much of it burnt out. Thankfully, nobody was injured.

Ingrid jumped in, "Worry about the future when the time comes."

I held Mary's hand between my own and asked if she was overwhelmed by Ingrid and me. Mary said it was alright, although knowing Mary, the planner, I knew she had to think about it. When resuming the talk about the possibility of Mary and me living together to save money, Ingrid said she could easily find another tenant in no time to replace her. Ingrid reassured Mary by saying if it didn't work out, Mary could quickly move out of my place. Mary told us to give her a few weeks to think about it.

By the second weekend of October 1981, Mary had decided to move into my apartment. Although it had one bedroom, a tiny galley of a kitchen, and one small closet, it was just big enough for us. Our living arrangements worked well. I took care of the cooking, and we studied together in between our classes on campus.

It was Tuesday evening, two days before Thanksgiving, when Mary's grandmother, Oma, originally from Germany, called Mary. Oma, grandmother in German, lived only a couple of miles away from Mary's family in Georgia. She told Mary, "Honey, I am looking forward to seeing you and your Lebanese lover for Thanksgiving. You know I love the Lebanese, and I knew Lebanese people when I lived in Germany. They are a lot of fun and clever."

Mary and I were thrilled. Mary gave me a high five as her grandma repeated that she loved Lebanese people. A few minutes later, Mary's father got on the phone.

"Well, as you heard from your grandma, you and your friend are welcome to come for Thanksgiving."

I loved the idea of eating turkey, as I had never eaten homemade turkey before. I focused on the concept of sitting among an American family at the same table, eating with them from the same dish. That image made me excited, and I hardly slept that night. My mind raced, spinning out fantasies of their house, what their furniture looked like, and what Oma, who knew a little bit about the Lebanese, was like. I wished she were in Daytona when I met Mary's parents.

Mary and I packed the car Wednesday afternoon and set out for Georgia. Along the way, I couldn't help but marvel at the construction of the bridges we passed over. Once I became an engineer, I realized I could design and build these remarkable structures. We arrived at Mary's parents' house by eight o'clock that evening. The whole family greeted us. Her father seemed to keep his distance, maybe weighing my intentions. In her early seventies, I extended my hand to Oma, Mary's grandma, but she pulled me in for a big hug. She said she already loved me from the way Mary had described me. Oma was soft-hearted. I could tell she was kind, open-minded, and laid back. Oma's behavior reminded me of my Arabic culture; therefore, I was immediately drawn to her.

Mark talked to me about his daughter, Abigail, and he favored her. I noticed that Abigail usually sat in the place of honor next to her father, whether it be in the family home or when we all dined at restaurants. I made it a point to talk about how intelligent and wise Mary was, how lucky her parents were to have her as a child, and how fortunate I was to meet her. I felt the whole family was awed, which surprised me. Mary's mom seemed pleased when I openly praised her eldest child.

Our Thanksgiving dinner was uneventful. I hardly spoke a word during the meal. I didn't want to rock the boat. I dutifully smiled and laughed at Mary's family jokes and comments, even though sometimes I didn't understand the American expressions. I kept a friendly face and agreed with everything they said for two days. Everyone was amiable; however, I was anxious to be home in Gainesville.

When Saturday rolled around, we drove back down to Florida. I was happy thinking about getting back to my routine and life with Mary.

15
RELOCATION TO WASHINGTON

WITHIN NO TIME, the fall quarter ended, and Mary and I did well in all our classes. The university changed from a quarter to semester system in the new calendar year. I didn't have money to pay for the winter semester, so I concentrated on tutoring students and doing yardwork. By mid-February 1982, I received a warning letter from the University of Florida for not attending school during the semester. They reminded me that my visa to stay in the U.S. was strictly a full-time student visa. Therefore, since I was not enrolled in school for that semester, U.S. immigration had the right to deport me.

I showed the letter to Mary. Her hands shook as she devoured the document. She asked me what I planned to do. I told her my best option was to escape to a bigger city. She asked, "What makes you think escaping to a bigger city will solve the problem?"

I reminded her, "The U.S. immigration knows

everything about me now because I have a record with the University. But if I leave Gainesville, nobody would have a record of me."

Mary suggested we talk to Ingrid. Our older friend was visibly sad and concerned for us as she read the letter. She advised against moving to New York or Chicago. She said those cities were too large and dangerous for me. Without any friends or family, she feared I would be lost.

Ingrid explained that, unfortunately, she did not have the financial resources at that time and couldn't help me for the summer semester. Disappointed but grateful for her kind words of encouragement, Mary and I left Ingrid's house and drove around Gainesville. Mary asked if my dad was still in Saudi Arabia or Lebanon. I told her he was not in Saudi Arabia and wasn't in Lebanon. The last time I tried to call him in Saudi Arabia, I explained to Mary, I was informed he was no longer there. When I called her a couple of months earlier, Mama also told me she had no idea of my father's whereabouts. I told Mary, "Perhaps my other option would be to go to immigration and explain my situation. Maybe they could give me special permission to work while I go to school." Mary didn't care very much for that idea. She thought if I went to immigration, they would deport me back to Lebanon without blinking twice.

Two months later, I received a second warning letter. This time it was not from the university but the immigration office. They wanted an explanation for why

I wasn't enrolled in school for that semester. Mary and I discussed the letter. She said if immigration came after me, she would tell them she was planning to marry me. Her reaction surprised and encouraged me. I wasn't sure if immigration would buy this.

I felt torn apart by my new life in America, trying to survive and build a future without financial means and what I would face in the Arab world if I were sent back – most likely being forced to join a militia.

As spring approached, I had more landscaping work and more students to tutor. I was making good enough money but still had to send much of it back to Mama and my sister in Beirut. I had been sending money to my family for the last several months, as my dad had stopped supporting them financially when he stopped mailing me funds. They still hadn't heard a word from my dad and hardly had any money to live on. I worked through the whole summer, as well, and received two more warning letters from the University and the immigration office. This time the letter was harsh, and the word "deportation" was mentioned.

In June of 1982, Israel invaded Lebanon. My country turned into a ball of fire. I tried calling Mama many times to see if she and my sister were still alive or not. I had no way of reaching them. I didn't know if it was the phone lines or if they were dead. My heart ached. Here I was in America, the country that supported Israel with all its resources, yet Israel was bombing the life out of my country – the home of my Mama, sister, relatives, neighbors, and friends. I felt like a traitor, ashamed and awful that I was in love with an American woman and was starting to fall for America. How could this be when America was supporting Israel in invading Lebanon?

By August, with the help of Ingrid, Mary, and my income from yardwork and tutoring, I was able to enroll at the university again as a full-time student. Ingrid invited us to dinner. As we were enjoying our meal, Ingrid asked about the possibility of Mary and me getting married as a way to get out of this mess. I had mentioned marriage to Mary before as an alternate solution. She was hesitant, but I felt Mary and I were destined to be together; a marriage now would accelerate the process. Being the logical person she was, Mary had a hard time wrapping her head around this notion. She said it could happen in time, but we were still struggling students with uncertain futures. Mary felt we needed to establish ourselves and give our relationship time to see where it was headed.

Three months after Israel invaded Lebanon, in September of 1982, the Lebanese president-elect Bachir Gemayel was assassinated. He was the only hope for the Lebanese to end the civil war and for peace to prevail between the Lebanese factions. With Bachir gone, my hope for my country's future was chopped to pieces. After Gemayel was killed, Israel occupied Beirut. The news about Lebanon was horrible, and I still had no way to find out the status of my mom and sister. I felt part of the hell burning in Lebanon sat inside me. Soon after, the United States, French, and Italian peacekeeping forces arrived in Beirut. I told Mary that the West now occupied Lebanon, and I might as well say goodbye to my beautiful country.

In early October, as we sat in Ingrid's living room sipping coffee, the subject of Mary and me getting married came up again. Ingrid said if Mary and I decided to get married, we should do it right away while I was a full-time legal student meeting the immigration requirements. On October 28, 1982, with shaky knees but in love, Mary and I went to the Gainesville courthouse to have a civil ceremony performed. Mary, the logical one, felt more like she was doing me a favor by keeping me out of a potentially dangerous situation. We had nobody with us except each other. We agreed to keep our marriage secret, except for Ingrid. Shortly after receiving the marriage certificate, Mary and I drove to Jacksonville and met with the immigration authorities. After filling out paperwork and interviewing us separately, the immigration authorities informed me that in three months, I would receive a permit letter to work in the U.S., which I did.

Mary and I went out to dinner to celebrate. Although we were having a lovely evening, Mary gently reminded me that she married me to help me and simply would not be able to, or be comfortable with, marrying anyone in the true sense without her family being there.

"But Mary," I said, "when I married you, I married you for life. I married you because I loved you. I did not marry you for convenience."

Mary decided to spend Christmas with me. Our Christmas was quiet, but we were both happy. I went out and cut down our first Christmas "tree." Our "tree" was a huge cedar branch I found on the grounds of a local hospital where I jogged each morning. It wasn't exactly fancy, but it was ours all the same.

Mary was delighted when she saw me enter the house with the monstrous branch. She laughed and said I could have been arrested if I had been caught. Mary was very diligent and advised me to live conscientiously in the U.S.

Mary also taught me the importance of respecting "time." Being from the Arab world, I had a different perspective on time. Mary kept a mental record of all the times I was late and how late I was. One night in July, when I showed up on Mary's doorstep two hours late, she appeared with a very long, serious face and sized me up with sharp eyes, telling me she wanted to cancel the date. She was sick and tired of my chronic lateness. Mary said I was being disrespectful and insensitive regarding her time and feelings. I tried to explain that time was not always so important in my culture, especially when it came to meeting up with friends. Mary told me I lived in the U.S. now, and time was critical, regardless. When I saw how serious and hurt she was that evening, I told her I would never be late again. And when I saw how earnest she was about our "tree," I promised never to steal a tree branch again.

Though I thought my actions harmless, I knew Mary was right deep down. It had been to Mary's credit if I had gained any wisdom. Mary was always more deliberate and wise, unlike me, who was spontaneous, instinctive, fearless, and heart-strong. It was no surprise to me why I had been drawn to this woman. She had all the qualities I lacked. I was delighted and fascinated by the smallest things that made Mary her own person. I couldn't believe she made a list before going grocery shopping. I was surprised when Mary folded her clothes before putting them in the chest of drawers, unlike me, who shoved my clothes, unfolded, into any crevice I could find. Although Mary told me this was a gender thing, she taught me how to be neat and organized, words that weren't in my dictionary.

In the first week of January 1983, Mary and I went to bid farewell to my three Arab friends. Sola, Lena, and Fadwa, who graduated, were going back to their country. It was an emotional moment for me. I would miss them very much. They were among my first friends in the U.S. and helped me transition into American life while still maintaining some trace of my Arab culture.

The winter semester was Mary's last. That semester we studied particularly hard. Mary's dream was to get a job as an economist in Washington, D.C. She had always been an ambitious woman. In the meantime, my dream was to get additional work in the summer as a landscaper so that I could pay my tuition for the fall semester.

In April 1983, a suicide attack on the U.S. Embassy in Beirut killed 63 people. This was the same embassy I visited to apply to the U.S. to study. Some who were killed were just like me, applying to come to the U.S. to study. I was devastated by the grim news. Mary and Ingrid were great support during this most difficult time.

Just a month later, in May, Mary finished her graduate school program. She received her Master's degree in economics with all coursework towards a Ph.D., but without a dissertation. I was so proud of her, but at the same time, I was afraid of losing her, as I knew she would be looking for a job soon. By August, an opportunity came up, and she received a job offer to work for the government in Washington, D.C. I kept telling myself I would go with her. Mary and I said little about the status of our living arrangements after she left Gainesville; I think we were both uncertain. However, a couple of weeks before Mary left, we were having dinner together in our apartment when she apologetically said that she needed to move to D.C. by herself to start with. She needed to find her way alone to continue growing and becoming independent before making a lasting promise. I was crestfallen. I asked her what had happened to our commitment, our marriage. Mary responded that she would always care about me, always be my friend and that I understood and appreciated her more than almost anybody, but our marriage had only been a way to help me through a tough time. She said if we were meant to be together, it would happen, and, at least, we would still be friends like before, but just long distance. Although her words were painful, I loved her too much not to respect her feelings and decision. However, part of me hoped that she might change her mind once she got there.

In September, I helped her move to Washington, D.C., feeling lost while I drove Mary north to her new home. Together we found an apartment for her and bought some furniture from the Salvation Army. I stayed with Mary for a week until her apartment was almost fully furnished. We spent much of that time exploring the neighborhood and finding grocery stores and shopping centers.

The following weekend, Mary and I went to the Shenandoah Valley to celebrate her birthday, as it was her first in the Washington D.C. area. It was a perfect weekend. We dined, danced, and hiked. The valley had beautiful rolling hills. Green, thick trees, lush flowers, and the towering mountains made me feel close to God when I climbed them. The smell of the flowers and trees took me far back to Ein Eble, except this time I was riding in a car instead of on a camel or horse.

On our last night, Mary and I held each other and cried. I did not want to leave Mary for a second, but I had no choice but to respect her wishes. I felt Mary was moving forward successfully in her life while my life was sitting still. I began telling myself she deserved a better person, a man as successful as her. Even though the shadow of sadness surrounded me, I had to accept the idea of being away from Mary and decided I might need to move on.

The following day, Mary drove me to the airport. She asked me to call her every night. I felt my heart was broken on the plane, knowing Mary was alone, knowing how awful loneliness was. I told myself that at least she knew the language and was not in a warehouse.

When I arrived at my apartment, I ran to the phone, dialing like mad, wanting to hear Mary's voice. When I said, "Hello, sweetie!" I was happy to listen to her sounding good and anxious to start her new job. We talked daily, and Mary appeared to be settling in and getting used to her new position. Meanwhile, I was missing her terribly. I missed wrapping a blanket around her when she was lying on the couch watching TV. I missed rubbing her head at night to help her sleep, and I missed making love to her.

One night after talking with Mary on the phone, I stayed wide awake in bed, thinking I was right back where I started in Gainesville. All my close friends had left except for Ingrid. The following day, I struggled with my job at the discount department store. I had been there ever since my work permit had been issued by the immigration authorities back in January. It was evident to my co-workers that something was wrong. My eyes were a nasty shade of red, and my head felt stuffed from staying up all night.

When my shift was over, I bolted from the store and drove directly to Ingrid's house. I wanted to talk to somebody who knew us. She couldn't help noticing the tears welling in my eyes. Ingrid hugged me and said, "Mary won't find anyone similar to you, Nabil. So stop being sad. I wouldn't be surprised if Mary doesn't call you to tell you she is now sure of you in a few months."

Ingrid's words were like a salve giving me renewed confidence. When I went home, though, the absence of Mary permeated the apartment. I began to think it would be best if I worked double shifts every day to keep myself busy since I wasn't going to school that semester. I was also focusing on saving money to send back to Mama and my sister.

When I walked into the store the following day, I asked my manager if he would be kind enough to let me work two shifts that day. He asked me, "Why?" I told him, "I am too lonely without my girlfriend." He laughed at me, told me to get a grip and find another woman. Part of me wanted to punch him, but I knew I'd lose my job.

A couple of weeks after her move, Mary called in the evening after returning from work. She was crying, saying, "I'm not sure I made the right decision." She said she was so lonely. She didn't know anyone in the city, and none of the neighbors knew her name. I calmed her down and told her it was not easy to move to a new place. I added that I really loved her, and maybe we were meant to be together. She asked me how I was so sure. I told her it was something I knew from the second I met her. Mary told me she wasn't as confident, but she felt we had a special connection.

She told me she wanted me to come to Washington, D.C. to be with her. She said she missed the way I cared for her and the adventures we had shared. She asked if it would be possible for me to be there in the next few days. My heart thumped explosively against my rib cage. I wanted to be with her more than anything else in the world. I told her I would leave Florida as soon as possible. She asked me how soon. I answered I could go in a couple of hours. She let out a yelp, thinking I was joking. I assured her all I needed from my apartment was my clothes and plants.

As soon as I hung up the phone, I went to my landlord. I told him Mary wanted me back, and I planned to move to Washington. He asked me if I was giving a month's notice. I told him I was giving him an hour's notice. He thought I was crazy to drive all night to Washington. He added that I would lose my deposit for not giving enough notice. I didn't care. I didn't care about anything except getting to Mary as soon as possible.

I hurried back to my place, filled the Pinto, Mary's old car, with my clothes in oversized trash bags and plants, and drove to work. I told my manager about my plans, and he also thought I had lost my mind. He wished me luck in the end and told me to keep in touch. Without a map or even directions to Mary's place, I left Gainesville at 11 PM and sped up the highway heading north towards Washington. It was six o'clock in the morning the next day when I called Mary, collect, from a rest stop in Selma, North Carolina, and told her I was on the way. Mary was speechless but ecstatic. She told me where she would leave the key to her apartment.

I arrived at Mary's place at around two o'clock in the afternoon. The sight of the messy kitchen was like finding an oasis. Right away, I happily fell into my domestic role. While I cleaned, I made Mary's favorite dish, a mixture of beef, rice, onion, and stew. A couple of hours later, Mary called to see if I had arrived. She was thrilled to hear my voice. I told her I was in the middle of cleaning and cooking her favorite dish. "Yakhni!?" she asked excitedly.

Once I finished cooking, I drove the Pinto to Mary's office. Mary fell between my arms. I joined her in her tears. Once we got to her apartment, we embraced tightly and danced. I felt like the happiest man on the planet.

A week after moving in with Mary, I secured two jobs. One was at a department store during the day, and the other was at a convenience store during the evening shift. The locations were very convenient, a mile from Mary's apartment.

Around this time, another tragic incident occurred in Lebanon in late October. The peacekeepers' headquarters in Beirut experienced a deadly attack that ended in killing 241 U.S. and 58 French troops. Mary and I both shed tears over this sad day.

I tried calling Mama and Jehan to check on them but had no luck. The last time I spoke with them was a month before leaving Florida for Washington, DC. I had been overjoyed to reach Mama and Jehan by phone. They said they were okay, but their neighborhood had been shelled, and there was much damage on their block. So, now with two new jobs in Washington, I continued to support Mama and my sister financially but had no time to go back to school.

A few months later, in March of 1984, during the same week, the American troops were pulled out of Lebanon as peacekeepers. Mary suggested I write immigration to investigate the status of my green card. When I asked her why she was so anxious, she said that although it would be difficult for us, it would be best to initiate a divorce after receiving my green card to start a new chapter together and see where it took us. After all, our marriage had not been shared with anyone, and for Mary this wasn't proper or valid and made her feel guilty. She assured me that she loved and cared for me, but she wanted to be ethical.

In early 1985, I finally received my green card. Mary and I had a very romantic dinner in Old Town Alexandria by the water that same week. She was adorable and practical, as always. Her voice faltered when she said since I had my green card, it would be better for us to go forward with the divorce. At around this time,

Mary and I agreed that I move out, as we needed to see if our friendship blossomed into something real for both of us. However, we would see each other frequently, but not on a daily basis. She told me she wanted to be certain I was the right man for her, particularly since she had little dating experience.

In the meantime, I developed a friendship with one of my male co-workers, Eric, at the department store. He and I started to spend time together, and he introduced me to some of his friends and family. My friend's family considered me like one of their sons in no time. The Cook family became my new American family. Every time Mary visited her family for a holiday, I spent my holiday with the Cooks. I thought of Eric as a brother and his sister, Tania, as my own sister. I even called his parents "Mama" and "Dad."

Eric's mother, who worked at a hospital in the Washington area, advised Eric and me to fill out applications for hospital work, as there were many openings. I liked the idea, especially when I found out the hospital salary exceeded the department store's salary. After putting in several applications, I got a job in the hospital as one of the housekeeping staff. I loved the new position. I changed my work at the convenience store to daytime hours and worked at the hospital in the evening. With the extra money I made at the hospital, I saved and sent more money to my family in Lebanon.

I was quickly promoted to a medical records clerk and then to a pharmacy technician position while keeping the daytime convenience store job. My salary continued to increase significantly with each promotion.

A couple of months passed with Mary and I giving each other space, however, we ultimately found we were hopelessly drawn to one another. Mary had called to ask if I would meet her for dinner at the Washington, DC marina. We shared an alfresco meal on the Potomac River. The full moon shone on Mary's face, making her eyes brigher than the stars dotting the sky. As I told Mary silly stories to make her smile like in the past, all of a sudden she interrupted me, as she had something to share. My heart almost stopped. I had no idea what Mary might say. I had already implanted in my mind that I wanted Mary to be happy, no matter what she decided to do regarding our relationship.

Mary looked at me with penetrating eyes. With a soft voice, softer than a baby bird's feathers, she said she could never find anyone like me. She told me I was her best friend and understood her better than anyone. She said we had an extraordinary bond. I explained that despite working two jobs, I never stopped thinking about my dream of becoming an engineer one day and having her in my life.

One night in February 1987, while watching the TV news, I heard that Syrian President, Hafez Assad, had sent troops into Lebanon that attacked the Lebanese Christian militia. Lebanon turned into a mass of fire again. I was heartbroken when I heard the news that the Syrian army was attempting to occupy East Beirut, the Christian sector where Mama and Jehan lived.

Shortly after, I met Ashley at work in the pharmacy department. She was much older than me and became another good friend. Ashley was a sister figure to me. She lived a secluded life, was very religious, and had only a couple of good friends. She was very close to her family. I introduced Ashley to Mary. Mary instantly liked Ashley as much as I did. The three of us began to hang out together, and we became very close. Mary and I told Ashley about our history together—how we met in Florida and moved to the D.C. area. Ashley was one of the kindness people I had ever met. She assured me that the right thing would happen with Mary and me in the end. She told me everything happened for a reason.

In October of 1989, I heard news reports that the Taif Agreement had been reached to provide the structure for ending the civil war and returning to a more normal, sound government in Lebanon. The agreement was negotiated in Taif, Saudi Arabia, where Baba used to work and was designed to end the fifteen-year-long Lebanese Civil War. It reinstated Lebanese authority in Southern Lebanon, which Israel had occupied, and set two years for Syrian withdrawal.

A few days later, my Baba called me out of the blue. I had not heard from him in the last few years. He said he had been in Mafraq ever since the last time we spoke on the phone. Baba informed me he desperately needed money and asked me to send him several thousand dollars at the earliest opportunity. His voice rang inside my heart; refusing his request was not an option. I went to the hospital credit union to see if I could take out a loan; however, they told me they could not provide me with the amount I requested. I would need a co-signer—another hospital employee. Ashley immediately agreed to be my co-signer, and I was very grateful to her to be able to help my dad.

While working two jobs, I decided to take one engineering class each semester, including Strength of Material and Engineering Dynamics, third-year classes. Somehow, I found time to study in between my jobs and was able to pass both classes.

The civil war in Lebanon ended in 1990, and the government and businesses in my country were restored. My sister began working for the government, which meant she and Mama didn't need me to send them money anymore, as they could make it on Jehan's salary. By then, I had saved enough money to allow me to quit my job at the convenience store and work only part-time at the pharmacy. I couldn't wait to become a full-time engineering student.

16
FINDING MY OWN 'AMERICAN DREAM'

IN JANUARY 1991, I became a full-time civil engineering student and moved back in with Mary. I worked ten hours a week in the pharmacy. After the winter semester ended in May, I increased my hours in the pharmacy from ten to 40 a week since I was not going to school. During the summer, Mary and I met a couple who lived in the same condominium building. The man, Danny, was short, with a stocky build, thick black hair, and glasses, and his girlfriend, Julie, was petite with light brown hair and blue-green eyes. We became very close friends and played doubles tennis and dined out regularly. Soon after becoming friends, they told us they were Jewish. When I was younger, I never could have imagined the day would come when I would call a Jewish man a brother, and a Jewish woman, my sister.

The love and warmth I felt from Danny and Julie were the same I felt from my Arab friends I met in

Florida and close friends and relatives during my child-hood. Danny and Julie took me back to my Arab culture and customs. We listened to Arabic music, belly danced, and moved to other traditional Lebanese dances while I drummed on my durbakeh. Everyone appreciated when I made Lebanese food, including hummus, baba ghanoush, kafta, and molokhia.

One night we all decided to go to Julie's place for a cup of tea. While sipping our tea, my thoughts took me back to the planes hijacked in the Jordanian desert a couple of decades ago. Danny noticed I was looking at him deep in thought, and asked me if everything was alright. I told him it could have been him, Julie, your dad or mom, or your brother or sister. The room became quiet except for my voice.

Julie asked me what I was talking about. I said, "You could have been on one of the planes."

Danny asked me what planes. I said the ones hijacked in Jordan back in 1970 by the Palestinian militias. When I was a young boy, I opened up and told them, I grew up hating you and all Jewish people. I learned the words "I hate the Jews and Americans" before I learned how to say "I love you, Mommy." And here I was now in love with the most unique and beautiful woman who was American, and my best friends were Jewish.

I continued, "I have to admit, when I first came to this country, I was torn apart trying to adapt to the American way of life, yet keep my Arab traditions and beliefs I learned as a child intact." I explained that this transition had been extremely difficult and confusing.

I related the story about my two little friends who were killed by shrapnel from an Israeli air raid and the Israeli pilot's arm tossed between the Mafraq young men like a ball. Danny stared at my face as if he had just seen a ghost. Julie, with teary eyes, asked me for a hug. Mary told them my childhood was very different than hers. While she never went to bed hungry, I had done so often. Mary indicated she could never imagine having children brought up in hate for other nations or peoples. Danny walked toward me. He and I embraced, and Danny said it was time to do something about this and change the world to become a better place. Of course, it was a rhetorical statement, but Danny meant it in his heart. And I immediately agreed with my beautiful Jewish friend and brother.

The fun summer of 1991 ended so quickly. It was filled with love and happiness from Mary, Ashley, Danny, and Julie. In the fall semester, I went back to school. Even though the classes were challenging and needed much attention, Mary and I still managed to see our friends between school and work, making me content and forget my school stress. I spent my Christmas holiday working overtime in the pharmacy. My supervisor periodically gave me special projects to maximize my work time during the holiday, which meant more income. The winter semester of 1992 was my last semester before receiving my engineering degree, and I began feeling more hopeful. Mary and I started talking seriously about our future together.

Once May arrived and I graduated with a civil engineering degree, I was the happiest man. I thought how lucky Americans were; anybody could work and go to college to improve their status in life. If I was able to do it, and English was not my first language, then anybody could do the same. Mary kept reminding me I was living the "American Dream." I had gone from being a housekeeper to a medical records clerk to a pharmacy technician, and here I was about to become a professional engineer. This type of opportunity would never have happened in my homeland. I fell more in love with America and its people.

Danny and Julie had a celebratory dinner for me. Our friends were as delighted as I was when I finally achieved my goal. It was hard to believe that these were the people I wanted to destroy when I was a little boy in Mafraq. I asked myself, how could a child grow up to hate people they had never met before? Would I have been the same person I am now if I never met my sweet Mary and dear friends? Should I have not left the ALF, would I have been six feet under somewhere in Mafraq by now?

I secured a job as a professional civil engineer with a government agency designing and building bridges, a wish fulfilled. Mary had worked as an economist and finance manager in the D.C. area since 1983.

I still had the nagging feeling that I needed to tell the world that love always wins over hate. I thought about writing a book to begin to change people's mindsets and show them the light instead of the darkness. I also wanted to let Americans know how an Arab child could easily be pulled into a current of hate and distrust.

Although Mary's family, especially her dad, was concerned about our relationship, Mary told her parents she planned to go to California with me for a two-week vacation in the summer. Her parents weren't pleased with our news. However, Mary's brothers determined that as long as their sister Mary was happy with me, they were happy for her.

The night before Mary and I went on vacation, Mark called and tried to convince Mary not to go on vacation with me, as he thought I might propose to her. He reminded her I was from a different country and background, and our marriage would be difficult. Mary's dad said that his parents were from two different cultures, and although they said they cared for each other, they fought a lot. It was hard for Mary to hear these words. She told her dad once he started to know me, he would like me.

When Mary hung up the phone, she was clearly hurt and upset. Mary reminded me that, at first, our road would be tough and challenging, but later on, when the family knew me better, they would start to accept me. She said they needed a chance. I gathered Mary into my arms, telling her not to worry. I said I would only marry her and not marry her family. This made her smile and I knew we would be able to face anything together.

The following day, Mary and I boarded a plane to San Francisco. The day after we arrived, I had a surprise for Mary. We went to a quaint cafe, and had a delightful lunch. Afterwards, I suggested we go for a drive. I drove toward the hospital where Mary was born. A couple of blocks away, Mary remarked, "That's odd, I was born in that hospital over there."

I acted nonchalantly. "What a coincidence."

Mary was even more surprised when I pulled into the parking lot. When she asked, "Why are we here?" I said, "I have something to do. Why don't you come in with me?" I saw a glimmer in her eyes. I think she was catching on to the surprise. We walked into the hospital hand in hand. I kept my eyes peeled for the labor and delivery department. Spying the floor number, we took the elevator to that department. A receptionist and nurse greeted us, asking if we needed help. I immediately responded, "No, we're okay."

"Are you here to visit relatives or friends?" the nurse asked.

"No, not really."

"What are you doing here?"

I said, "Wait and see." She looked at me wonderingly. I put my hand in my pocket, picked out Mary's engagement ring, went on my knees, and proposed to her. Mary said yes, and I almost fainted. The nurse and receptionist were stunned, and they couldn't help crying when Mary started to tear up. I explained that my princess was born here, and I wanted to start my life with her in the same place where she came to life herself.

The nurse congratulated us and took some pictures. As Mary and I headed out to the car, I apologized for fooling her. She said she had fooled me first. She had a feeling about what was happening but enjoyed her special surprise. We drove to Big Sur that day, celebrating our engagement in that breathtaking area.

A few days later, we visited Mary's Native American relatives from her mother's side. They were very warm to us and welcomed me into the family. I felt so close and connected to them, like they were my Lebanese tribe. We stayed with them for a few days.

As we flew back to Washington, my love was worried. I kept my arm around her the entire plane ride, assuring her everything would be fine. I said I was willing to pick up the phone when we went home, call her family, and ask them if we could visit. She loved the idea. She told me, "If Sadat was able to make peace with the Jews, then you can make peace with my family."

I told Mary I would do anything for her as long as I lived and as long as it made her happy.

The minute we got home, we both got on the phone to call her parents. They were shocked to hear my voice but remained polite and respectful. I was even surprised when they congratulated us on our engagement. A week before Thanksgiving, Mary got a phone call from her parents, inviting both of us to Thanksgiving dinner.

Feeling a mixture of anxiety and excitement, I told Mary that I would like to go.

The dinner went very smoothly. Her father asked me many questions about my job, goals, and plans. Although some of his questions were too forward, I pretended not to mind. I answered each one with a smile and a calm demeanor. Part of me understood Mark's position; he loved his daughter very much and wanted to be sure she would marry the right man.

Mary said she hoped every visit was as pleasant as this one as we flew back home. I had explained to Mary that in Arab culture, sons-in-law and daughters-in-law were instantly treated as members of the immediate family. The "American way" was something I needed to get used to. Some elements of the American culture fascinated me, and others were unsettling, just like any other culture in our world.

In January of 1993, Mary and I agreed to get married on Labor Day weekend. We decided to bring Mama from Lebanon to northern Virginia to attend the wedding. Preparing all the necessary paperwork for a visa was the easy part. Mama had the more demanding job: traveling to Damascus, Syria, to obtain a visa from the U.S. Embassy because the Embassy in Beirut was closed due to the civil war. Mary and our wonderful friend, Julie, worked diligently over several months to ensure the wedding would be memorable. My adopted Jewish brother, Danny, kept reminding me how proud he was of me for becoming a civil engineer and soon to be marrying an amazing woman.

In the summer of 1993, I called Baba to invite him to my wedding in September. Baba paused for a second and asked if I was in Lebanon. I told him I was in Washington, D.C. I hardly finished my sentence when Baba asked who I was marrying. When I said she was an American, my Baba was beyond angry at me. He told me if I married an American woman, he would prefer to die than see me again. He reminded me that marrying a person outside my culture was wrong and shameful. He claimed my soul had transformed into a devil since I moved to the U.S. He said his shame for me was depthless. Before hanging up the phone, Baba told me he would never forgive me for marrying an American. I felt sad about my dad's behavior; however, I couldn't change his mind.

Planning for the wedding was stressful, but Mary and I were glad to have a wedding instead of eloping as we had initially planned. It was Mary's father who encouraged us to have a traditional wedding. He said, "A wedding will be something that you'll always remember and will allow all your friends and family to join in the celebration of your marriage." I was surprised by his suggestion and enthusiasm, but it did make a lot of sense to us. His sensitivity and caring were incredible.

Mary and I were delighted when we heard from Mama the first week of August. She had been granted a visitor's visa to attend our wedding. Mary and I drove to Dulles airport to meet Mama during the last week of August. My legs were unsteady, and my heart pounded relentlessly against my chest. Mary assured me everything would be okay even though I hadn't seen Mama in fifteen years. Mary's words gave me courage. I felt like I could meet Mama and control my emotions. Mama's diabetes had blinded her in one eye, and she had only limited vision in her other eye. She was also recovering from hip surgery. I made arrangements for her to come in a wheelchair.

Mama's plane landed, and we began watching passengers come down the gangplank. We became concerned when the last passengers disembarked without a sign of Mama. Mary and I approached the gangplank, but security would not allow us to enter. We decided to sit outside in the waiting area. Ten minutes passed like ten days.

"I don't think she's coming. Something must have happened," I said. Mary put her arm around me.

"Just sit tight. I know she will be here soon." As she finished her statement, we saw a wheelchair coming down the gangplank pushed by airline staff. I jumped up from my seat.

"That's Mama!" I yelled excitedly. I took hold of Mary's hand and began running toward Mama. Mary collapsed beside me, crying uncontrollably. My fiancée, who had supported me and given me the power to suppress my emotions, now needed my support. I held Mary tightly, telling her everything would be alright. I asked Mary to calm down and greet Mama. Tears streaked our faces as we raced together toward Mama.

Mama heard my voice and yelled back, "Nabil, Nabil!" Once we reached her, the three of us hugged and shared each other's tears. It was one of the most emotional moments in my life. Minutes passed by, and Mama, Mary, and I were still embracing and sobbing. I greeted Mama in Arabic and asked her about her long trip. Between her tears, Mama said everything was fine. Her dream had come true to see me once again before she died. I asked her about my sister, Jehan, and Mama said we needed to call her soon because she was so worried about Mama traveling the long distance alone.

As Mama and I spoke, Mary held Mama, kissing her face and telling her she loved her in Arabic. Mary had learned some Arabic from me during the many years we spent together.

In the car, I sat in disbelief that the woman beside me was my real Mama. I did not feel the same connection towards her as I had felt during my years growing up in Jordan and Lebanon. I held her hand while I drove, wanting to smell it, to remember and feel bound to her, again. I kept looking at her face, examining it, still foggy that Mama was really here. I had fifteen years of news that I wanted to share. I needed to know how she lived every day without me. I asked Mama so many questions; there was barely enough time to get them all in.

Mama was exhausted after her grueling trip, so we

didn't stay up too late. I felt sad when she informed me that one of my aunts passed away from cancer, and a couple of our neighbors in Beirut were shot dead during the civil war. Mama reminded me that the Syrian army had bombed our kitchen and burned half of it. The kitchen had just recently been repaired. I listened to her while my body trembled. My left arm stayed protectively around Mama while Mary draped her right arm over Mama's other shoulder.

The following day Mary and I took Mama to several malls in our neighborhood. She was in a wheelchair due to her recent hip surgery and was tired due to her travels, but she was impressed to see and learn about the American way of life. We also introduced her to our friends, including our Jewish buddies, Danny and Julie. Mama ended up falling in love with them. Even though Mama did not speak a word of English, she understood and communicated with all our American friends through smiles, eye contact, and gestures.

Three days before our wedding, Mary's parents arrived from Georgia. It thrilled me to see how well Mary's parents and Mama got along. Mary's mother made sure Mama was comfortable and well-fed at all times. Two evenings before the wedding, Mary's mom told me Mama strongly reminded her of her own mother. She told me she felt connected to Mama as if she had always known her. Although the two women could not speak to each other, I could tell they bonded. Mary's father, known for his exuberance and loud presence, was extremely polite and kind to Mama.

The day before the wedding was busy and was taken up with the rehearsal. All of Mary's family and some of her relatives arrived from all over the country. We had asked Danny and Julie to be in the bridal party, and they gladly accepted. I explained to Mama that the rehearsal was an American tradition, an event preparing for the wedding. The Lebanese culture does not have a rehearsal before the wedding ceremony.

As Mary and I exchanged vows during the rehearsal, I teared up. Mama began crying, too, and rose from her seat, walking to us. She asked me, "Honey, are you okay? If this is a rehearsal, then why are you crying?" I couldn't explain it to her, and I could only embrace her. The words Mary and I expressed during the rehearsal had been the feelings planted twelve long years ago.

During the rehearsal dinner, Mary's father made a memorable speech that made me respect him more despite the uncomfortable feelings we'd shared in the past. He conveyed his admiration for me and how I brought Mama all the way from Lebanon for the wedding. Later, he said he realized how Mary had become happier and more complete than she'd ever been. I went to his seat when he finished, hugged him, and planted two kisses on each cheek without thinking. He was caught off guard, and some chuckled at my forwardness. He stood up, put his arm around me, and looked at everyone.

"Don't be surprised," Mark said. "This is how we do it in Lebanon."

I appreciated this gesture.

The wedding ceremony went perfectly as planned. Mary looked breathtaking in her wedding gown. I felt faint when Mary's father walked her down the aisle toward me. Lebanese culture dictates that the parents of the bride bring the daughter to the groom's parents, and they bring the bride to the groom. I was not surprised when Mama began walking toward Mary and her father to receive the bride. Ashley walked behind Mama quickly and grabbed her, taking her back to her seat.

During our wedding reception, I watched Mary's father dance with Mama, treating her as if she were a member of his own family. It filled my heart with pride and love for both of our families.

Not long after we cut the cake and toasted with several glasses of wine, I heard a different type of music echoing in the hall. It sounded Lebanese, much different from the Beatles and Chicago music we danced to all night. At first, I blamed it on the wine, taking me back to the music of my home. As I thought deeply, trying to discern if the music was real or imaginary, Mary came to me and asked, "Honey, how do you like the belly dancing music? The Lebanese music?" I hugged her fiercely, happy I wasn't drunk. I was excited to see Mama dance with Mary's father to the Lebanese music of her native land. As Mary pulled my hand to the dance floor, we moved to the Lebanese music, Mary using the belly dancing techniques she learned from me over the years. Everyone joined in and danced to the music of my homeland.

The next day, Mary and I flew to Portugal for our honeymoon. Mama stayed with Ashley while we were gone. After two weeks, we arrived back to the D.C. area refreshed and appreciative of spending an additional month and a half with Mama before she returned to Lebanon in late October. We were gratified to take her to doctors for her diabetes and her eyes. It was lovely to wake up in the morning and see Mama preparing a healthy, home-cooked Lebanese breakfast of eggs and pita bread with olives, labneh, zahter, and pickled egg-plant on the side before we went to work. Mama spoiled us as if we were little babies.

From the moment Mama met Mary, she looked at her like she was one of her own daughters. I remember when Mama and I called Jehan and Sonia a few days after Mama arrived in America. Mama told my sisters that Nabil's fiancée was one of the best people she had ever met, and Nabil was one of the luckiest men to be marrying someone like her. Jehan answered, "If Nabil and you love her, then she is part of our family, and we shall love her as a sister." Jehan admitted in Arabic, and I had to translate to Mary, that she and Sonia never thought America would have a woman good enough for their baby brother. Still, they were mistaken and asked Mary to forgive them. My sisters gave Mary an open invitation to visit Lebanon. On Mama's departure day, we promised her that we'd visit her in the next few years.

In October of 1993, a month after we were married, we bought a five-bedroom house not far from our condominium. We were living the typical American life in suburbia. As I gardened and trimmed the grass with my electric lawn mower, I reflected on how I cut other people's lawns in Gainesville to survive and continue my schooling. I always envied those people, and now I was one of them. Our neighborhood community was diverse with people of varying ancestries, as was all of America, unlike Lebanon or Jordan. We became especially close to a Jewish family and spent a lot of our free time together.

One morning at the breakfast table, Mary and I talked about how intriguing and unlikely it was that Jewish people had become some of our dearest friends. It struck me that Arabs and Jews lived a similar lifestyle filled with hospitality and generosity since ancient times. I told Mary no wonder I felt so attached to our Jewish friends.

My sister, Ida, called me from Jordan the third week of May 1995 and said our Baba had liver cancer. I was devastated to hear the news. I still loved him as much as a son could love his father. I asked Ida about the best time for me to see him. She told me the best time would be after he died. She told me Baba didn't want to see me. I was leveled; my sister's honest answer tore my heart out. I kept in touch with Ida while Baba was in the hospital. As his condition worsened, I was devastated and angry at myself. I wasn't sure exactly why I felt upset and disappointed, but these emotions plagued me.

A couple of weeks later, Ida called to tell me Baba was gone. When she asked if I was planning to come to the funeral, I paced, silent for a few minutes, and finally told her it wouldn't do any good. Even though Baba left this world, I felt that I became closer to his soul. I often saw him in my dreams and talked to him, even in my daydreams.

Christmas of 1996, Mary and I followed up on our promise to Mama and visited her in Lebanon. Even though Mary was a bit worried, I assured her it would be alright, as Lebanon had no current war threats. As we flew over the ocean, I asked God to give me the strength to handle all I was about to experience healthily, as it had been many years since I left home. We stopped in Jordan to visit my father's grave on our way to Lebanon.

The feeling I had when I approached Mafraq was incredible. I felt happy and sad at the same time. It brought me to my childhood memories. The first thing I looked at was Mafraq's sky as if I was searching for Israeli planes. The second thing I looked for were young men carrying guns. Mafraq looked completely different after 21 years. I visited the house where I was born. I showed Mary the place where the ALF headquarters and Latin Church had stood. I pointed out the spaces where the church walls had been, the walls that hid me during the Israeli air raid. I showed her the soccer field I had played on when I lost my two little friends. It was a bittersweet feeling, mostly bitter. I considered myself lucky, though, to have had a childhood filled with rich memories.

We flew from Amman, Jordan, to Beirut. Entering the city, I was alarmed to see many buildings either fully or partially destroyed, some with large holes from shelling and rocket fire, remnants of Lebanon's Civil War. It had been 18 years since my last visit. The feeling in Beirut was quite different from the feeling in Mafraq. I had been in Beirut for only two years, and during that time, I lived amid a bloody civil war. In Beirut, however, I had people who I cared for and were still alive. In Mafraq, the only thing left for me was my father's grave. I had no way of knowing what happened to my friends there.

Mama and Jehan were euphoric to see Mary and me. Jehan treated Mary like a sister as if she had known her since childhood. Our visit to Lebanon was a series of celebrations, day and night. My relatives and the neighbors were enlivened, almost overwhelmed over having us there. They transfixed us with their dancing and transformed my wife into a more natural belly dancer.

Our time in Lebanon passed much too quickly. The last night was extremely sentimental. I sat on the very same brown sofa just before I launched my journey into the unknown on that Christmas Eve of 1978. At that time, I was filled with confusion and anxiety before leaving Lebanon for the U.S. AGAIN; here I was, but now in my thirties, an engineer and living the "American dream." This time I was leaving with contentment and a peaceful mind with my American wife to my life on the other side of the world.

ABOUT THE AUTHOR

NABIL KHOURI built a successful career in engineering after emigrating to the United States at the age of 19. After marrying his American-born wife, Mary, they settled in the Southern United States. Nabil Khouri does a variety of volunteer work within his community that includes advancing interest in, and knowledge of, Middle Eastern culture. He loves traveling internationally with his wife.

Lightning Source UK Ltd.
Milton Keynes UK
UKHW011021070223
416609UK00006B/1360